AF293623

O THOU THAT HEAREST PRAYER

Pray and create *Possibilities*

O THOU THAT HEAREST PRAYER

Pray and create *Possibilities*

ALAIN LUBAMBA

Print: Libri Plureos GmbH, Friedensallee 273,
22763 Hamburg (Germany)

© Alain Lubamba, 2024.
Publishing : Blossom Publishing Inc. – www.editionsblossom.com
ISBN : 978-2-9822016-8-2

Legal deposit: 4th quarter 2024.
Bibliothèque et Archives nationales du Québec
Library and Archives Canada

Author: Alain Lubamba Mbuyi
Literary direction: Aurélie Nseme Obiang
Graphic design: Aristide Benameyi / Benameyi Graphiste
Revision and corrections: Éditions Blossom Publishing

Lord Almighty, I am deeply grateful for the strength and inspiration you have given me to bring this dream to life. Just as drops of water fill a vessel over time, you have poured revelation after revelation into my heart throughout our journey, shaping this meaningful tool for the ministry and the perfecting of the saints.

CONTENTS

ACKNOWLEDGEMENTS

To my beloved wife, Nana Lubamba, and our children: Jeffrey Lubamba, Joy Lubamba, and Jaimely Lubamba, you hold a special place in my heart. Nana, you have been my prayer companion and a remarkable prayer partner from the very beginning. I affectionately refer to you as my personal intercessor, second only to the Holy Spirit. I will forever cherish your guidance during our devotional times.

To my dear mother, Cecile Mbelu, a remarkable woman who has always entrusted me with matters concerning God's kingdom. I am proud to be your son and deeply grateful for your unwavering prayers, encouragement, and support in prioritizing what matters most: loving and serving God at all costs.

To my dear Aunt Antoinette Kapinga, who departed to be with the Lord many years ago; this book stands as a testament to your fervent prayers. It also honors the cherished memories of your invaluable advice on the importance of commitment and prayerfulness for the glory of God, and the advancement of His Kingdom.

To Pastor Michel Kamanda and Dr. Birland Lo-sambola, my esteemed companions in ministry and prayer partners, I fondly recall our humble beginnings with great enthusiasm. Together, we navigated through challenging conditions during personal retreats, tirelessly pushing God's agenda forward, in the territory assigned to us for ministry. Our memorable moments of prayer and powerful times of administration will forever be engraved in my heart.

To the late Pastor Vernaud, the Patriarch, I owe you a debt of gratitude for the teachings you imparted, enabling me to weather the storms in both my life and ministry. Your wisdom and guidance still resonate within me, shaping my journey and strengthening my determination. May God bless you abundantly, Sir.

To Apostle Dalo Luhata, as a mentor and role model, your unwavering commitment to cultivating an extraordinary prayer life remains a beacon of inspiration in our hearts. Your tenacity and steadfastness have left a permanent mark on our lives. We are profoundly grateful for your guidance and invaluable advice.

To Apostle Veyi, I am immensely grateful for being a beneficiary of the grace of God upon your life. Your exceptional leadership style has profoundly influenced the La Borne Church Youth Ministry for many years, leaving an enduring legacy of faith and impact.

To all my brothers and sisters in the Lord who have ministered alongside me for the past 39 years, your dedication and support have been invaluable. As prayer partners in all seasons, we have journeyed together, sharing both joys and challenges. Your unwavering support amidst difficulties is deeply appreciated.

To all my translators and proofreaders—Pastor Roland Dalo, Pastor Leticia Komba, Pastor Didier Kahungu, Sister Nana Lubamba, Sister Sylviana Nsumbu, and Brother Patrick Mays—I extend my heartfelt gratitude for your unwavering availability and contributions to this project. Your dedication and support have been invaluable.

Finally, my deepest appreciation goes to the Times of Champions and DGG Church, particularly the daily morning prayer sessions led by Dr. Rhema Ngoy, a tremendous blessing to the body of Christ. May God bless you abundantly for the countless blessings I have received through your ministry, and for the privilege of serving alongside you in Canada and across the globe during revival and outreach meetings.

FOREWORD

Thirty-six years ago, in His foreknowledge, Jehovah placed on my path a young man barely out of his teens who had just had his encounter with Christ. I remember it as if it was yesterday (because it seems to me as if the days have flown by) and again, I can see his attire, his face – he was a little shy and quiet, but above all, his thirst and desire to get to know the One to whom he had just entrusted his life.

That is how I first got to know the author of the wonderful book you are now holding in your hands. Since then, many things happened: our initially somewhat shy relationship has grown much stronger since, in addition to the spiritual influence I've had on him, we've also worked together at the Centre Evangélique et Francophone de La Borne in the Democratic Republic of the Congo, where he's done great and efficient work in his field – that of management.

When he sent me the manuscript of this book, I thought to myself: «Yet another book on prayer.» But very quickly, on each page of «Oh Thou that hearest prayer,» I not only repented but also found myself saying: «This book must be published and read by the largest number of Christians,» for several reasons; here are five in particular:

1. Its wealth in presenting this important and predominant activity for every child of God: prayer.

2. Its style, which is at once detailed and elaborate, yet simple and consumable for all generations of God's children.

3. It teaches us not only what prayer is but also the do's and don'ts of prayer.

4. It spares us from adding to the extensive list of people whose prayers are not answered, not because of the One they are praying to, but because of the way they practice this spiritual exercise, and especially because of the wrong foundations. The apostle James says in James 4:3 (KJV): **"You ask and do not receive, because you ask wrongly...» (I like the Word of Life translation which says: you ask and receive nothing? Because you ask wrongly..."** Therefore, it is not enough to practice prayer; we also need to know the basics and how to pray effectively.

5. The author's didactic and pedagogical approach. With 40 years in the Lord and almost 33 years of pastoral ministry, rarely have I read such a terrific book about prayer. Therefore, I encourage you to read «Oh Thou that hearest prayer» and make sure others read it, for it is worth the try.

May God bless you.

Your brother in the harvest, Roland Dalo, Servant.

INTRODUCTION

God is waiting for your prayer and has answers in store for you before you even engage in a prayer session. Whether you decide to pray or not, **«The biggest loss isn't on the part of the One who controls the whole universe; rather, it's on your end, as you miss out on the most vital and exciting platform that keeps you connected to the Father, who eagerly awaits an ongoing conversation with you.»**

Becoming aware of a God (Elohim) who is attentive when you address Him through the conveyance of prayer will change and affect your day-to-day journey of faith on Earth. Your prayer is your access code to the throne of glory. That is why you can boldly say in accordance with 1 John 5:14 (KJV), **«And this is the confidence that we have in him, that, if we ask anything according to his will, he heareth us.»** Indeed, he will hear you when you decide to start a conversation with Him.

In fact, prayer has been a driving force for Christianity in every generation and season of believers' lives. It has served as a focal point for many decades, and what a remarkable mystery it is. Generation after generation has produced generals of God's ministry who have sought Him with great commitment through effective prayer. They have maintained an outstanding prayer style and achieved great results to the glory of God.

The amazing lesson behind these wonderful scenes of victory is the fact that many of them established simple but powerful prayer principles that justified their consistent and successful walk with the Lord our God every day of their lives.

Amazingly, these individuals come from various ages and generations, yet they all share numerous truths that we can still claim and reproduce today for a more rewarding prayer life.

But why should we publish another book like this? The answer to this question can be found in the book of the prophet Daniel. He wrote under the inspiration of God's Spirit: **«But thou, O Daniel, shut up the words, and seal the book, even to the time of the end: many shall run to and fro, and knowledge shall be increased.»** Daniel 12:4 (KJV)

Prayer is a mystery. God is raising a new generation eager to witness more of His presence in their lives. They understand that God's word is the source of knowledge, and faith in Him produces miracles, among other blessings. To live victoriously, Christians with strong Christian values should cherish and nurture a prayerful lifestyle.

The Holy Spirit is on the move, empowering generations through various means to fulfill their mandate. As the Church moves closer to the rapture, prayer becomes more crucial than ever. There should be an awakening of urgency, motivating us to build capacity in prayer to remain relevant in our time and aware of what is about to unfold.

That is why this book on prayer is an expression of a heart that desires God, providing another opportunity to share how much can be accomplished by increasing awareness of our God, who is ready to hear our prayers. His attributes reveal how powerful and capable He is. As you continue to press on and discover who He is and what He can do, it becomes vital to explore the space available to grow in knowledge of Him and experience the grace received through interacting with Him.

Jeremiah 33:3 (KJV) says : «**Call unto me, and I will answer thee, and shew thee great and mighty things, which thou knowest not.**»

The Bible states that the things mentioned above are for our instruction, teaching, and example so that we do not follow the same destructive path and drift away from God. Instead, we gain knowledge of the principles and understand the promises and prophecies to apply for a successful life, even amidst the challenges under the sun.

E.M. Bounds aptly said,

«Prayers don't die, they don't fade. They outlive the lives of those who have uttered them.» He also reminds us that *«Nothing is done well without prayer for the simple reason that it takes no account of God.»*

«The Word of God is the fulcrum on which the lever of prayer is placed, and by which things are powerfully moved.»

A committed Christian must continually attend to his or her own prayer life, while understanding that prayer goes beyond religious practice and generation; it becomes a lifestyle. Take your prayer life from an emergency room to a true modus operandi throughout your days; elevate and sustain your prayer ministry.

In the New Testament, Jesus reveals that our Father God is a great and attentive listener and that He answers prayers. We hear Him pray in:

John 11:42 (KJV) - **«And I knew that thou hearest me always: but because of the people which stand by I said it, that they may believe that thou hast sent me.»**

A praying Christian is eager to pray; he believes the Father hears him when he prays (Psalms 65:2). Let this book ignite your prayer life and bring you closer to Him with great assurance.

PART I

Psalms 94:9 (NIV) - **«Does he who fashioned the ear does not hear?»**

«*This is allowed to be an unanswerable mode of argumen-
tation. Whatever is found of excellence in the creature must
be derived from the Creator and exist in Him in the pleni-
tude of infinite excellence.*»

Adam Clarke's Commentary on the Bible

I.

APPROACHING HIM AS A FATHER

God is our Father. Our relationship with Him is secure enough that we can trust Him and approach Him safely without fear. However, many believers approach God with a sense of bondage and guilt. The life of our Lord Jesus Christ exemplifies God's fatherly character: «Let the little children come to me» and «pray to the Father.» He is the exact representation of God's being.

Matthew 6:9-13 (KJV) : **"After this manner therefore pray ye: Our Father which art in heaven, Hallowed be thy name. Thy kingdom come. Thy will be done in earth, as it is in heaven. Give us this day our daily bread. And forgive us our debts, as we forgive our debtors. And lead us not into temptation, but deliver us from evil: For thine is the kingdom, and the power, and the glory, forever. Amen. For if ye forgive men their trespasses, your heavenly Father will also forgive you: But if ye for-**

give not men their trespasses, neither will your Father forgive your trespasses.''

The Lord Jesus taught us to pray using this model as a guide. It was a framework He provided to instruct His disciples on how to approach prayer. He said, 'When you pray, start like this': «Our Father» (Abba in Hebrew, meaning source, defender, support). You must approach God with reverence and pray with a deep understanding of the Father's revelation.

Indeed, He is the source of everything. One of the main characteristics of a father is that he is a «GIVER». God is not an adult child; He is a Father who gave us His own Son.

Jesus highlighted that even flawed earthly fathers know how to give good gifts to their children. How much more, then, will our heavenly Father—abundant in love—provide whatever we ask for, according to His will. Therefore, let us come to God with great assurance and a clear understanding that He is a provider who freely gave us Jesus Christ.

Reflect on God's incredible ability to listen every time you speak. He is the greatest listener you have ever met and will ever meet during your earthly experience. Reflect on His powerful attributes, which enable us to deepen our understanding of His divine nature and elevate our prayer life to a level of deep awareness in Him, the author and finisher of our faith. Prepare to transform every prayer opportunity into a powerful moment that yields the desired results.

The Father that hearest

God hears and is ready to answer; all we must do is ask according to His will and wait upon Him in prayer.

As our Father, God has good things in store for us, as it is written, «Eye has not seen, nor ear heard, nor have entered into the heart of man the things which God has prepared for those who love Him» (1 Corinthians 2:9).

Romans 8:15-16 (KJV) : **«For ye have not received the spirit of bondage again to fear; but ye have received the Spirit of adoption, whereby we cry, Abba, Father. The Spirit itself beareth witness with our spirit, that we are the children of God.»**

On our earthly journey, we have been given a remarkable spiritual tool that allows us to stay connected and communicate with our Creator, God the Father, the source of all things. This tool is prayer.

The Hebrew language contains many words that convey the concept of 'prayer'. We will discover these words as we progress through this book. In general, prayer is translated from the Hebrew language as «PALA», which means to interpose, entertain, or dialogue. Indeed, it is a reliable means of communication that connects man on earth with God in heaven.

God delights in communion and communication with mankind.

Effective communication is fundamental to every relationship. It is a skill that is highly valued across all areas of life, whether between couples, within families, or at every level of an organization—from local management to national governance. Communication is key to building and maintaining healthy relationships. It's important to recognize that God, above all, values communicating with us, making it a priority in our connection with Him.

The author of Genesis illustrates this truth in the dialogue that takes place in the Garden of Eden.

Genesis 3:8-10 (KJV) : **«And they heard the voice of the LORD God walking in the garden in the cool of the day: and Adam and his wife hid themselves from the presence of the LORD God amongst the trees of the garden. And the LORD God called unto Adam, and said unto him, Where art thou? And he said, I heard thy voice in the garden, and I was afraid, because I was naked; and I hid myself."**

Initially, God delighted in constant communication with mankind until they encountered the serpent in the garden, leading to the unraveling of everything. Following that pivotal event, communication with God was disrupted, and a period of silence ensued. It was not until many years later, with the birth of Enosh, that people began to call upon God once again.

Genesis 4:25-26 (KJV) : **«And Adam knew his wife again; and she bare a son, and called his name Seth: For God, said she, hath appointed me another seed instead of Abel, whom Cain slew. And to Seth, to him also there was born a son; and he called his name Enos: then began men to call upon the name of the LORD."**

At that time, men began to call on the name of the Lord. From that moment, humanity rediscovered and reignited its sincere desire to converse with and rely on the Creator. They returned to the foundational principles that God had taught them in Eden, recognizing that God was an essential part of their journey on earth.

The word «invoke» originates from the Greek «epikaeomai» (επικαλέομαι), which means "to pray", "to invoke". It is translated into English as to:

- Ask, to seek help from someone, especially a god, when one wants to improve a situation.

Psalms 138:3 (KJV) says, **"In the day when I cried thou answeredst me, and strengthenedst me with strength in my soul."**

The word «invoke» also carries the meaning of:

- Making someone feel a particular way or reminding them of something.

Psalm 57:2 (KJV) says : **"I will cry unto God most high; unto God that performeth all things for me."**

The word «invoke» can also mean to:

- Appeal to or invoke authority.

Nehemiah 2:5 (NIV) says : **"and I answered the king, 'If it pleases the king and if your servant has found favor in his sight, let him send me to the city in Judah where my ancestors are buried so that I can rebuild it.'"**

The word «invoke» also encompasses the idea of:

- Appealing with longing or making supplications, especially in praying for something such as God's mercy.

2 Samuel 14:11-12 (KJV) says : **"Then said she, I pray thee, let the king remember the LORD thy God, that thou wouldest not suffer the revengers of blood to destroy any more, lest they destroy my son.**

And he said, As the LORD liveth, there shall not one hair of thy son fall to the earth. Then the woman said, Let thine handmaid, I pray thee, speak one word unto my lord the king. And he said, Say on."

Jesus exemplified outstanding communication when He responded to the disciples' request to learn how to pray. He gave them clear and concise instructions, guiding their understanding of what prayer truly entails. He described the proper disposition for prayer as being directed toward the Father in a clear and simple manner, making our communication both appealing and captivating to His heart. In doing so, Jesus highlighted the importance of ensuring our prayers are relevant and fruitful, fostering meaningful interactions with God. He further explained that a lack of response or interest from the Father might be attributed to ineffective or poor communication on our part.

Approaching God boldly and confidently, and understanding that He listens and takes pleasure in communicating with us, will profoundly change your perception of prayer.

In Hebrew, to listen (hear) means **«shama»**. It signifies listening attentively to someone's request and providing them with an answer.

In the case of Hagar, Abraham's concubine, who had fled into the wilderness after being mistreated by her mistress, Sarah, the angel of the Lord appeared to her. He assured her that God had heard the cries of her son, Ishmael, in the wilderness. The angel instructed Hagar to return to her mistress and promised that she would give birth to a son named Ishmael, signifying «the God who hears when I cry» (Genesis 27:15-20).

Genesis 16:15-16 (NIV) : **"So Hagar bore Abram a son, and Abram gave the name Ishmael to the son she had borne. Abram was eighty-six years old when Hagar bore him Ishmael."**

Jesus Christ also mentioned the God who always hears when we pray.

John 11:40-43 (KJV) : **"Jesus saith unto her, Said I not unto thee, that, if thou wouldest believe, thou shouldest see the glory of God? Then they took away the stone from the place where the dead was laid.**

And Jesus lifted up his eyes, and said, Father, I thank thee that thou hast heard me. And I knew that thou hearest me always: but because of the people which stand by I said it, that they may believe that thou hast sent me. And when he thus had spoken, he cried with a loud voice, Lazarus, come forth."

Indeed, both the prophet Isaiah and the psalmist recognized God as the One who hears and responds to prayers.

Isaiah 65:24 (KJV) : **"It shall come to pass that before they call, I will answer; And while they are still speaking, I will hear."**

Psalms 4:1 (KJV) **: "…Hear me when I call, O God of my righteousness: thou hast enlarged me when I was in distress; have mercy upon me, and hear my prayer."**

The moment of manifestation is within God's jurisdiction.

While the Father hears our prayers, it is essential to recognize that the timing of their manifestation is in God's hands, which affirms His sovereignty. As Christians pray, they often anticipate answers that align with their preferred timing, which may not necessarily coincide with the best time or manner according to God's plan.

The answering of requests brought to God's knowledge serves as evidence of His omniscience, omnipresence, and complete sufficiency. God can hear the prayers of His people simultaneously and from any place, demonstrating His boundless awareness and presence. He intimately knows the personal and intimate needs of everyone, discerning what is best suited for them.

God is a remarkably attentive listener, particularly attuned to what is communicated to Him. His capacity to listen surpasses our comprehension. As widely acknowledged, individuals who possess the skill of attentive listening are highly esteemed; indeed, it is among the foremost qualities sought after in any leader.

Malachi 3:16 (KJV) : **"Then they that feared the LORD spake often one to another: and the LORD hearkened, and heard it, and a book of remembrance was written before him for them that feared the LORD, and that thought upon his name."**

The preceding passage underscores that while those who feared Him pondered their situation in comparison to the unrighteous, God heard their words. In fact, God attentively listened to the words of their mouths and subsequently chose to intervene.

A good listener is valued for several reasons, including:

- **Concentration:** A good listener fully concentrates on what the speaker is saying, engaging with their ideas thoughtfully and thoroughly.

- **Commitment to Understanding:** They do not just hear the words; they commit to digesting the information presented and responding constructively.

- -**Emotional Awareness:** A good listener is attuned not only to the words being spoken but also to the underlying feelings, emotions, and intentions conveyed in the conversation. They listen with both mind and heart.

- **Empathetic Engagement:** To be an effective listener, it is crucial to first tune into the speaker's frequency by putting yourself in their shoes. This conveys the message: «I'm listening, I'm interested, you have my undivided attention. Please, continue.»

Consider the immense power of your relationship with the Almighty God, who undoubtedly resonates with the frequency of the words you speak during your prayer session. **God not only embodies all the qualities of effective listening described earlier but also transcends what the human mind can comprehend as the utmost capacity for attentive listening.**

Most books on prayer tend to focus on the mechanics of prayer—how to pray, who to pray to—rather than delving into a deeper understanding of the secrets of God, particularly His role as the 'God who hears prayers.'

1 John 5:14 (KJV): **«And this is the confidence that we have in him, that, if we ask any thing according to his will, he heareth us."**

Often, we find ourselves dominated by the spirit of doubt, questioning whether God truly hears our prayers or engages in our conversations. Throughout Scripture, we encounter numerous examples of individuals grappling with similar doubts. Even King David, as reflected in his words below, expressed these same fears.

Psalm 22: 1 -2 (KJV) : **"My God, my God, why hast thou forsaken me? Why art thou so far from helping me, and from the words of my roaring? O my God, I cry in the daytime, but thou hearest not; and in the night season and am not silent."**

When we say 'God hears your prayer,' it signifies that God eagerly awaits our dialogue, our requests, and our conversations with Him. It implies that He is already prepared to respond, indicating that our unspoken requests already have pre-established answers in the economy of God's kingdom.

It is no surprise that Elijah, a man just like you and me, prayed. I am convinced that Elijah possessed a revelation about prayer that granted him assurance or a deep understanding of its potential when following the protocol of the kingdom, praying to God the Father. He knew that consistent prayer would prompt the Lord of hosts, who resides amid praise, to hear him and address his requests in due time.

He hears men, and all flesh will come to you.

The Greek origin of **'to hear**,' which is **'Akouo,'** is prominently used in the Scriptures. It carries a deeper connotation than mere auditory perception, signifying not only hearing but also responding and obeying.

We are encouraged by God's ever-present availability even before we turn to Him. Let us approach Him boldly and without fear, recognizing that we, as people of all nations, encompassing different ranks, conditions, and circumstances, have unhindered access to the throne of grace. Through Jesus, the Mediator, who has opened the way for anyone turning to Him in repentance and genuine contrition, we can become children of God and citizens of His kingdom.

Zechariah 8:21-23 (KJV): **"And the inhabitants of one city shall go to another, saying, Let us go speedily to pray before the LORD, and to seek the LORD of hosts: I will go also. Yes, many people and strong nations shall come to seek the LORD of hosts in Jerusalem, and to pray before the LORD. Thus saith the LORD of hosts; In**

those days it shall come to pass, that ten men shall take hold out of all languages of the nations, even shall take hold of the skirt of him that is a Jew, saying, We will go with you: for we have heard that God is with you."

This is the confidence we have in him: if we ask anything according to his will, he hears us (1 Jean 5:14-15).

"How amazing is the assurance conveyed in this verse, which states, 'If we ask our heavenly Father anything according to His will, He hears us."

It is evident that the Lord has heard us when we pray for our loved ones' salvation, the restoration of marriages, deliverance from addictions, or healings and miracles in alignment with His promises and plans.

Yet, despite our prayers, we may encounter disappointment when our requests remain unanswered or unfulfilled, causing our spirits to wonder if the Lord has truly heard us. In these moments, we may question what happened or if we missed something.

Beloved, when we place our trust in the Lord, we do so with all our hearts, recognizing His sovereignty and trusting in His perfect timing. However, when our heartfelt desires attempt to mask themselves as His will, it is essential to reevaluate our prayers.

When we grasp the truth that the Lord's ways are higher than ours and His thoughts surpass our understanding, we will learn to pray as our Lord Jesus did in the Garden of Gethsemane:

"**...remove this cup from me: nevertheless, not my will, but thine, be done.**" (Luke 22:42).

We serve a living God, and we are confident that none of our sincere prayers will go unnoticed. He is El-Shama, our God who hears us when we call. Let us always have the assurance and boldness that He has already heard us even before we utter our needs to Him.

Approaching God boldly and recognizing that He delights in hearing our prayers will deeply impact our relationship and enhance our intimacy with Him. Changing the way we pray is crucial for maintaining a vibrant prayer life and ensures victory over life's challenges. We are grateful for the trust we have in our Heavenly Father.

Psalms 66:17 – 20 (KJV) : "**I cried unto him with my mouth, and he was extolled with my tongue. If I regard iniquity in my heart, then the Lord will not hear me: But verily God hath heard me; he hath attended to the voice of my prayer. Blessed be God, which hath not turned away my prayer, nor his mercy from me!**"

II.

THE EXCLUSIVE ATTRIBUTES OF GOD

The Scriptures illuminate the character of God, revealing His attributes and nature. As we immerse ourselves in His Word, our understanding of Him deepens, leading to a desire to learn more about Him. This knowledge transforms us, shaping our personal lives and influencing every aspect of our being.

Jesus Christ played a pivotal role in facilitating this transformation by intervening and sealing the reconciliation that restored our relationship with the Father. Through His life, teachings, and sacrifice, Jesus impacted our perception of God, leading to a deepening of our prayer life. He revealed God to us in a simple yet profound way, making the divine accessible and relatable.

John 14:9 (KJV) : **"He that hath seen me hath seen the Father**."

John 5:38-39, John 14:9 (NIV) : **"Nor does his word dwell in you, for you do not believe the one he sent. You study... Jesus answered: "Don't you know me, Philip, even after I have been among you such a long time? Anyone who has seen me has seen the Father. How can you say, 'Show us the father?"**

Our prayer life would be significantly enhanced if we learned about and gained awareness of the attributes of an amazing God. By delving into the administration of God's Word, we uncover deeper truths that highlight these attributes.

Take a moment to pause and reflect! Discovering more about God's attributes will undoubtedly add a gentle and sweet flavor to your love for prayer and deepen your connection with the One you pray to.

The Jews have a deep understanding of God's attributes, and when they call upon Him in specific circumstances, they address Him with this understanding. They believe that God will act in accordance with the attributes that define His power and manifestation. This truth can be articulated in human language to convey the depth of their conviction and understanding.

God has amazing attributes. What do they mean, and why is it important to know them? When we discuss God's attributes, we seek to answer questions such as: Who is God? What does God look like? What kind of God is He?

An attribute of God is something that is true about Him. While it is impossible for us, as limited beings, to fully understand who God is, He reveals Himself in numerous ways, both through His Word and His creation. Through these revelations, we can begin to grasp the nature of our awesome Creator and God.

God resembles nothing and nobody we know or can imagine. He is unique and beyond comparison. Even when attempting to describe Him in words, we fail to fully grasp what He is like—our language simply cannot do justice to our holy God.

Nevertheless, God has attributes that we can know, albeit only partially, and He has given us His Word as a light to enlighten us.

Throughout this chapter, we have explored some of God's attributes, which can be grouped into two categories: The first category consists of what some theologians call «exclusive» qualities—those that God alone possesses and that are reserved to Him. The second category comprises «inclusive» qualities—those that both God and we possess, but which only He possesses perfectly.

1. Self-Existence

This term describes an eternal being whose existence is not subject to the limitations of time. God is self-existent, infinite, and beyond our ability to trace His origin.

Psalms 90:2 (KJV): "**Before the mountains were brought forth, or ever thou hadst formed the earth and the world, even from everlasting to everlasting, thou art God.**"

Colossians 1:17 (KJV): "**And he is before all things, and by him all things consist.**"

These passages of Scripture confirm that God exists by Himself. In other words, He was not created by anything imaginable and has always existed.

Psalm 147:5 (KJV): "**Great is our Lord, and of great power: his understanding is infinite.**"

It is challenging for an ordinary person, within their limitations, to comprehend the nature of our limitless God. For instance, in the King James Version, the name «Lord God» is the English translation of «Jehovah,» which appears 6,800 times in the Scriptures. It reveals God's sovereignty, strength, and goodness. The attribute of «self-existence» refers to the One who has never ceased to exist and will always be.

What a blessing it is to understand that we belong to a self-existent God who created us in His image and likeness and that everything that has ever existed was created by Him.

2. Omnipotence

The quality of unlimited or immense power is known as omnipotence. God is omnipotent, possessing power in its entirety in heaven and on earth.

Matthew 28:18 (KJV): **"And Jesus came and spake unto them, saying, All power is given unto me in heaven and in earth."**

Psalm 33:6 (KJV): **"By the word of the LORD were the heavens made; and all the host of them by the breath of his mouth."**

All power rests with God, who is Himself the Almighty. The human mind has no capacity to fully describe the extent of this power; it is simply limitless. It is impossible for humanity to fully comprehend this mystery.

The word **«Omnipotent»** is a combination of two words: **«omni**,**»** meaning all, and **«potent,»** meaning powerful. Omnipotent simply means possessing unlimited power. No wonder the apostle Paul says:

"Now unto him that is able to do exceedingly abundantly above all that we ask or think, according to the power that worketh in us," (Ephesians 3:20), or **"Nothing is too difficult for God to accomplish"** (Jeremiah 32:17); God's word makes it clear: **"Who is this King of glory? The LORD strong and mighty, the LORD mighty in battle."** (Psalm 24:8).

He spoke to Job, saying:

"Where wast thou when I laid the foundations of the earth? declare, if thou hast understanding. Who hath laid the measures thereof, if thou knowest? or who hath

stretched the line upon it? Whereupon are the foundations thereof fastened? or who laid the corner stone thereof; When the morning stars sang together, and all the sons of God shouted for joy? Or who shut up the sea with doors, when it brake forth, as if it had issued out of the womb? When I made the cloud the garment thereof, and thick darkness a swaddling band for it.." Job 38:4-9 (KJV)

Who can oppose God?

The remarkable thing is that God's decisions in any situation will always be consistent with His character, and He has all the power to execute the plans He desires to unfold in any individual or on earth.

God's power can be overwhelming when you read the Scriptures; however, take comfort in knowing that He is consistent in everything He does. The only exception is that sin cannot be tolerated in His sight. The author of Hebrews 6:18 (NIV) portrays this reality in the following way: **"God did this so that, by two unchangeable things in which it is impossible for God to lie, we who have fled to take hold of the hope set before us may be greatly encouraged."** God cannot contradict Himself.

3. Unchangeability or Immutability

This expression means that there is no possibility of change in Him; in fact, God is immutable. Everything about Him remains constant, and there is no variation.

James 1:17 (KJV): **"But whatever is good and perfect comes to us from God, the Creator of all light, and he shines forever without change or shadow."**

According to the Cambridge Bible for Schools and Colleges, "God does not change His promises and purposes of grace (Romans 11:29); whatever rebellious ways His people, the Israelites, took, they were always preserved."

Malachi 3:6 (NIV): **"For I am the LORD, I change not; therefore, ye sons of Jacob are not consumed."**

God does not change; there is no variation in Him. He has not changed in the past, He does not change now, and He will not change tomorrow; He remains the same forever and ever. It is important to note that all of God's attributes remain consistent from before what we call the beginning of time to infinite eternity.

He is the only one with a character that never changes; there is no chance of God becoming worse or better than yesterday. The architecture of His thoughts never changes. What He has promised through His Word remains unchanged, regardless of the time and circumstances. He is always constant in everything. Now you see why you need to trust Him, I mean, trust in the result He can bring about when you pray.

With this aspect of God's unchanging divine nature, we understand that His portfolio of purposes and promises does not change. We can boldly, through our faith in Him, rest assured when we pray, despite our own fluctuations and sins. What incredible assurance for the believer to possess this fundamental thought of an unchanging God.

It is worth leaning on God in all things and in all circumstances. Our trust in God gives us the assurance that He will never fail us. We see that His promises are unassailable, and His purposes for our lives are unshakeable.

4. The God of omniscience is omniscient.

He knows everything.

Isaiah 46:9-10 (NLT): **"Remember the things I have done in the past. For I alone am God! I am God, and there is none like me. Only I can tell you the future before it even happens. Everything I plan will come to pass, for I do whatever I wish."**

He is aware of every moment of every day of your existence; he never slumbers or falls asleep. The exciting thing is that He can intervene anywhere, at any time. He knows our life, and He's always with us. There is not a single place on this earth where we can find ourselves that God does not see and is not aware of.

The fact that God is omniscient allows us to believe that He knows everything, from beginning to end, including what we are experiencing today and all that we will experience tomorrow.

When we spend time meditating on this truth through the mirror of His other attributes such as love and goodness, we will gain a true picture of the trust we have in Him, from the most important things to the most mundane and trivial aspects of our lives.

5. The God of omnipresence is omnipresent.

He is everywhere, always present, and at any time. It is essential to understand that there is a difference between God «being» in one place and us «being in one place». The concept of God's being "is quite different from the physical realm," as the website Ligonier.org explains.

Jeremiah 23:23-24 (KJV): **"Am I a God at hand, saith the LORD, and not a God afar off? Can any hide himself in secret places that I shall not see him? saith the LORD. Do not I fill heaven and earth? saith the LORD."**

Psalm 139:7-8 (KJV): **"Whither shall I go from thy spirit? or whither shall I flee from thy presence? If I ascend up into heaven, thou art there: if I make my bed in hell, behold, thou art there."**

"Where shall I go from your Spirit? Or where shall I flee from your presence? If I ascend to heaven, you

are there! If I make my bed in Sheol, you are there! If I take the wings of the morning and dwell in the uttermost parts of the sea, even there your hand shall lead me, and your right hand shall hold me."

The Psalmist affirms God's omnipresence.

Indeed, the awareness of God's omnipresence offers profound comfort to Christians facing loneliness and grief. By cultivating the knowledge that God is always present, we can find solace and assurance, knowing that we are never truly alone, regardless of our circumstances.

6. The God of self-sufficiency.

He is self-sufficient and has no needs.

John 5:26 (KJV): **"For as the Father hath life in himself; so hath he given to the Son to have life in himself;"**

God's self-sufficiency means that He possesses infinite riches of wisdom, being, goodness, and power within Himself (John 5:26; Ephesians 3:16).

This self-sufficiency stems from His ultimate perfection, which includes His complete knowledge and love as the Father, Son, and Holy Spirit.

As for limited humans, they have profound needs which, if left unmet, can lead to dire consequences, even death. However, God, in His self- sufficiency, has never lacked anything.

Understanding God's self-sufficiency should embolden us to approach Him with confidence, knowing that He is fully capable of meeting all our needs. This echoes the sentiment expressed by Paul in Ephesians 3:20 :

"Now unto him that is able to do exceedingly abundantly above all that we ask or think, according to the power that worketh in us…"

None of His children need to worry about depleting His boundless well of grace, kindness, mercy, and generosity.

III.

THE INCLUSIVE ATTRIBUTES OF GOD

God said in Genesis 1:26-27 (KJV) : «Let us make man in our image, after our likeness." The second group of attributes is considered inclusive, indicating that they are not exclusive to a particular group; these are attributes shared by both God and humanity equally.

1. The God of faithfulness is truly faithful. He is infinitely and immutably true.

The Hebrew word translated as «fidelity» denotes «constancy, faithfulness, steadfastness.» The antonym of faithfulness is fickleness or changeability.

Psalm 119:89-90 (KJV) says: **"Forever, O LORD, thy word is settled in heaven. Thy faithfulness is unto all generations: thou hast established the earth, and it abideth."**

Faithfulness here is equated with God's Word.

2 Timothy 2:13 (KJV): **"If we believe not, yet he abideth faithful: he cannot deny himself."**

Deuteronomy 7:9 (KJV): **"Know therefore that the LORD thy God, he is God, the faithful God, which keepeth covenant and mercy with them that love him and keep his commandments to a thousand generations."**

However, this raises the question of what God's faithfulness means concerning His covenant. God promised significant blessings to the Israelites (Genesis 12:1-3), and under the old covenant, the Jews rightfully associated divine faithfulness with the blessings He bestowed upon them.

You must understand that all of God's attributes are not isolated features, nor separate but interconnected parts of His perfect nature. No wonder the apostle John wrote: **"This is the confidence we have in him."** 1 John 5:14 (KJV).

All His attributes are interconnected; His faithfulness cannot be understood outside of His immutability. So, when we meditate and study the Word carefully, we discover that God remains faithful no matter what, because He cannot deny Himself. The fact that He is immutable means that He can never fail to be faithful.

The Word of Promise is certain. In all His dealings with His people, God is faithful. He can be safely relied upon. No one has ever trusted Him in vain. We find this precious truth expressed almost everywhere in the Word, for His people need to know that faithfulness is an essential part of the divine character. It is the foundation of our trust in Him.

The fact that God is unchanging and infinitely faithful means that He never forgets a thing, never changes His mind, never goes back on a promise, and never fails to do what He set out to do. Understand that His faithfulness flows from His love, as Paul affirms in the Word: «In all things God works for the good of those who love him» (Romans 8:28). Of course, we do not always see or understand how faithful His plan is.

Indeed, acknowledging God's faithfulness can be challenging, especially when faced with suffering and loss. In our limited understanding, His faithfulness may appear as abandonment. However, during such times, taking comfort in remembering God's attributes can provide assurance. Despite trials, we can trust in His immovable goodness, faithfulness, constant presence, and wisdom. Trust what God says, He remains a great source of comfort.

"For now, we see through a glass, darkly; but then face to face: now I know in part; but then shall I know even as also I am known." 1 Corinthians 13:12 (KJV).

2. The God of goodness is good. He is infinitely, immutably good, and full of goodwill.

It is written in Psalm 73:1 (KJV) that "Truly God is good to Israel."

Is God good? "Taste and see that the Lord is good" (Psalm 34:8, KJV).

Indeed, reconciling God's goodness with suffering can be challenging. During times of adversity, doubts may arise regarding God's ability to help or even His love for us. When life is going smoothly, it is easier to affirm God's goodness, but during challenging times, doubts may creep in. However, it is essential to remember that God's goodness is not dependent on our circumstances. Even amid suffering, His goodness remains constant, and He works for the good of those who love Him (Romans 8:28).

The psalmist invites us not only to believe that God is good, but also to experience his goodness.

King David's affirmation of God's goodness amidst suffering underscores a profound truth about the human experience. Despite the afflictions that the righteous may face, David acknowledges that God's goodness remains constant. This insight challenges us to trust in God's goodness even amid trials and tribulations.

Psalm 34:19 (KJV): **"Many are the afflictions of the righteous: but the LORD delivereth him out of them all."**

3. The God of justice is just. In fact, He is infinitely immutable, just, and perfect in everything He does.

Many people in this world are constantly asking what it means for God to be just. It is not just about being fair. It goes further and means that God is good to all mankind and always does what is right.

God is without injustice; He is faithful, just, and right. Naturally, we wonder how a God that is just can justify the unjust. Thanks to Christ's atoning work, justice is not violated but satisfied when God spares a sinner. His mercy does not prevent Him from executing his justice, any more than his justice prevents Him from executing his mercy. He is both fully merciful and completely just.

Considering God's other attributes of love, goodness, grace, and mercy, some might mistakenly say that God is too good to punish the sinner. But to believe this, is to ignore the reality of His infinite and unchanging justice.

4. The God of mercy is merciful. He is infinitely, immutably compassionate, and gracious.

In fact, the Hebrew word for mercy, **«rehamim,»** is the plural of «womb» and is related to the emotion of the womb. It is what a mother feels for the child she is carrying in her womb. Finally, «hesed» describes the covenant of loyal love. God is actively and inexhaustibly compassionate. His mercy is also undeserved.

Romans 9:15-16 (KJV): **"For he saith to Moses, I will have mercy on whom I will have mercy, and I will have compassion on whom I will have compassion. So then it is not of him that willeth, nor of him that runneth, but of God that sheweth mercy."**

As indicated under the previous attribute, God's mercy is inseparable from His justice. He is immutably, infinitely merciful - He forgives, He is unfailingly, lovingly good to us. This is indeed an undeserved mercy.

Without God's mercy, we would have no hope of heaven. Because of our disobedient hearts, we deserve eternal death. **"For all have sinned, and come short of the glory of God;"** Romans 3:23 (KJV).

Thanks to God's mercy, we do not receive what we deserve. Instead, through God's mercy, we receive life through faith in Christ. If we were to imagine a world without guilt, where there is no pain or tears, God would still be infinitely merciful, but His mercy might remain hidden within Him. It is human misery and sin that call for divine mercy.

If we imagine a world without guilt, where there is no pain or tears, God would nevertheless be infinitely merciful, but his mercy might well remain hidden within him. It is human misery and sin that call for divine mercy.

5. The God of grace is merciful.

God is infinitely inclined to spare the guilty. With mercy, we do not get what we deserve (damnation); grace consists in getting what we do not deserve (eternal life).

"The LORD is gracious, and full of compassion; slow to anger, and of great mercy." Psalm 145:8 (KJV).

Grace is not just an action he bestows, but part of God's identity, and that means we can trust in the eternity of grace.

"For by grace are ye saved through faith; and that not of yourselves: it is the gift of God..." Ephesians 2:8 (KJV).

His grace is also sovereign. **"...I will be gracious to whom I will be gracious..."** Exodus 33:19 (KJV).

Speaking of God's grace, Bible scholars and theologians often make a difference between God's saving grace and God's common grace. The basic definition of grace in Greek is ''unmerited favor'', an unmerited gift, a favor granted as a gift and given freely. In this sense, grace is a gift common to all mankind.

That is why everyone - Christian or not - enjoys the blessings of life, provision, and abundance.

Matthew 5:45 (KJV) tells us: **"...for he maketh his sun to rise on the evil and on the good, and sendeth rain on the just and on the unjust."**

This is an opportunity for the reader to know that while all mankind benefits from common grace, the same cannot be said for saving grace, which is exclusive to those men who profess, believe, and put their faith in Christ receive saving grace. This is what evolves in our sanctification and glorification of God, so that we can live for Him and enjoy Him for eternity.

6. The God of love is loving. God loves us infinitely.

Indeed, the attribute of love is foundational to God's character and is intricately connected to all His other attributes. It is eternal, sovereign, unchanging, and infinite, serving as the bedrock of His relationship with humanity.

"Beloved, let us love one another: for love is of God; and every one that loveth is born of God, and knoweth God. He that loveth not knoweth not God; for God is love." 1 John 4:7-8 (KJV)

God's love is dynamic, bringing us closer to him. He does not love humanity in a vague sense, he loves human beings. His love is personal. He loves you and me. And his love for us knows no beginning and no end.

7. The God of holiness is holy. He is infinitely, immutably perfect.

"Holy, holy, holy Lord Almighty" Revelation 4:8 (KJV).

The term holiness is used in reference to his otherness, his separateness, and the fact that He resembles no other being. It means revered, set apart, sacred, or divine. Yet none of these words is sufficient to describe the formidable holiness of our God.

It gives an indication of His completeness and infinite perfection. Holiness is the attribute of God that binds all the others together. Holiness is the only attribute that possesses the most unique description of God and reality, it is a summary of all His other attributes.

"Be ye therefore perfect, even as your Father which is in heaven is perfect..." Jesus says in Matthew 5:48 (KJV).

The fact that God is holy means that His standard for us is perfection, that He is ceaselessly, always perfect. Without Christ, who took our place and died for our sins, we would not measure up to God's holiness. That is why we need Christ.

Glory be to God, Christians will never have to experience God's holy wrath. Through Christ's death and resurrection, the price for our sins has been paid and Christ's righteousness imputed to us. Consequently, when God looks at us, He only sees Christ's holiness in its perfection, nothing less, nothing more. This is what allows us to stand in the presence of that which is divinely perfect and pure.

8. The God of glory is glorious. He is infinitely beautiful and great.

The first word, «glory,» is translated from the Hebrew word «kabod,» which conveys meanings such as: «weight,» «strength,» «power,» and «ability.» Additionally, «kabod» carries connotations of: «honor,» «magnificence,» «splendor,» and «dignity.»

This is an important concept in the Old Testament, about which there is much to say. Here is how the prophet Habakkuk describes it.

"And his brightness was as the light; he had horns coming out of his hand: and there was the hiding of his power." Habakkuk 3:4 (KJV).

This description is certainly apt and in keeping with what Scripture often describes of God's glory, as a dazzling light that shines brighter than anything we can experience on the face of the earth. No wonder Moses claimed to have witnessed Yahweh's glory.

One of the frequent errors of Christianity is to emphasize only one attribute of God and to believe that He is just "one thing." For example, many make the mistake of believing that God is love and nothing more. It is certain that God is love but at the same time he is also light, he is omnipotent, and he is holy - just to name a few. We must learn about the Person of God, and this can be done by studying his attributes which are revealed in his Word.

It is important to understand that there is not one attribute that is more important than another or that should be emphasized as more important. God is the totality of the attributes of His character and if we are to have a relationship with Him, we need to seek to know and love him as He is, not as we perceive Him with our senses.

The Word of God is our reliable source of information about God as our Father, so let us study it. We want to know God so that we can walk with Him. We must therefore study it deeply to increase our knowledge and combat ignorance (Hosea 4:8): "Now this is eternal life, that they know you, the only true God, and Jesus Christ whom you have sent."

IV.

RELATIONSHIP BETWEEN FATHER AND SONS

Prayer is indeed a dialogue between God and humans, a conversation that reflects the relationship between a loving Father and His children. Belief in God's existence and his attentive response to our prayers is foundational to the act of prayer itself.

"But without faith it is impossible to please him: for he that cometh to God must believe that he is, and that he is a rewarder of them that diligently seek him." Hebrew 11:6 (KJV)

God hears only the prayer of the righteous, not that of the sinner. However, in His sovereignty, He can intervene in the affairs of the entire world for all individuals, whether they are Christians, Jews, other believers, or unbelievers.

For God to care for someone, a father-son relationship must be established, which is only made possible through surrendering one's life to Jesus.

"The LORD is far from the wicked: but he heareth the prayer of the righteous." Proverbs 15:29 (KJV)

Prayer is about God and His children.

It is through prayer that we ask our heavenly Father to manifest powerfully in our daily lives. Prayer is a two-way street between Father and sons. Matthew 7:11 (NIV): **"If you, then, though you are evil, know how to give good gifts to your children, how much more will your Father in heaven give good gifts to those who ask him!"**

We are called to dominate; this is the mandate we received from God when He created man and woman in His image and likeness. Throughout the course of God's interaction with humanity, sin corrupted man, leading to God's turning away from him due to His hatred of sin. Yet, God introduced a mechanism by which He could restore communion (Koinonia) with man, as in the beginning.

He came down Himself, took on the form of a human being, and paid the price of sin by condemning it on the cross of Calvary.

As the Bible says: **"For all have sinned and fall short of the glory of God..."** (Romans 3:23).

By His own will and predetermined plan, He manifested Himself in Jesus, who walked on planet Earth and restored the broken relationship.

After fulfilling the sacrifice, He ascended into heaven and sent the Holy Spirit. Those who believe in Him become children of God. A deeper study of the Word reveals different statuses of children.

Do you know your status in the kingdom of God?

Interestingly, Christian development and growth follow basically the same pattern as human growth and development. One starts out as a baby, then a young child, then an older child, then a full grown adult and, finally, a parent. Although these stages of growth are almost automatic in a healthy human, it is not so in the spirit realm.

When speaking of a child in Jewish society, allusion is made to those who remain totally dependent on adults. In the New Testament, Jesus himself shows great admiration for children in whom he sees the type of disciples.

The aim of the apostle Paul's comprehensive teaching of the word of God was to bring everyone to the status of being «mature in Christ.» The word translated here as «mature» is the Greek word 'teleios', derived from 'telos', which means the goal, objective, or end for which something exists or is accomplished.

The Greek terms nepios, paidion, teknon, and huios are used to denote various stages of spiritual maturity. We begin as nepios (infants), progress to paidion (young children), then to teknon (spiritual adolescents), and finally to huios (fully mature sons).

We begin with the term «nepios» (infants), which is what the Apostle Paul says in 1 Corinthians 13:11 (NKJV): **"When I was a child (nepios), I spoke as a child (nepios), I understood as a child (nepios), I thought as a child (nepios); but when I became a man, I put away childish things."**

The new birth is a beautiful term describing the salvation experience. The moment a man is born 'from above' (John 3:3), it is said that he becomes a new creation in Christ Jesus our Lord. His spirit is filled with the Holy Spirit. He is a new spiritual baby, a babe in Christ.

The next stage of development is that of a young child, a PAIDION. The first thing we see about a PAIDION is that they are humble, Matthew 18:4 (LSG): "Therefore whoever humbles himself as this little child is the greatest in the kingdom of heaven." Indeed, this may be the characteristic that indicates a NEPIOS has begun to grow. They are to come unto their Lord. They have begun to intimately know their Father, as we read in **1 John 2:13 (NKJV) : "I write to you, fathers, because you have known Him who is from the beginning. I write to you, young men, because you have overcome the wicked one. I write to you, little children, because you have known the Father."** Think about a young physical child between two and ten years old.

They are not yet ready for the world, but they learn to love and imitate their parents. PAIDION learns to 'mimic' their heavenly Father (Ephesians 5:1). They are, or should be, also under the tutelage of a spiritual father (PATER) in the Church. Jesus called His disciples PAIDION (John 21:5), thus indicating their level of spiritual growth.

All who believe are given the power to become children of God.

Another word for «children» is translated from the Greek as «téknon»: A young person from birth to adolescent and his glossed as child or children in plural.

«Teknon» («a child living in voluntary dependence») clarifies how we are all to live in absolute dependence on the Lord at every moment, allowing ourselves to be guided, cared for, and nurtured by our heavenly Father. The emphasis is on the childlike, not childish, attitude of the heart that willingly submits to the Father's plan. We better understand how to be receptive to Christ, who speaks His rhēma-parole within to transmit faith,

Hebrew 5:12 - 14 (NKJV): **"For though by this time you ought to be teachers, you need someone to teach you again the first principles of the [b]oracles of God; and you have come to need milk and not solid food. For everyone who partakes only of milk is unskilled in the word of righteousness, for he is a babe. But solid food belongs to those who are [c]of full age, that is, those who by reason of [d]use have their senses exercised to discern both good and evil."**

Matthew 19:14 (NKJV): **"But Jesus said, "Let the little children come to Me, and do not forbid them; for of such is the kingdom of heaven."**

Romans 8:16-17 (NKJV): **"The Spirit Himself bears witness with our spirit that we are children of God, 17 and if children, then heirs—heirs of God and joint heirs with Christ, if indeed we suffer with Him, that we may also be glorified together."**

Transliterally, the Greek Teknon means:

A. τέκνον, τέκνου is related to offspring, plural children.

- In the strict sense, properly, universally.

1 Timothy 3:4: **"One that ruleth well his own house, having his children in subjection with all gravity."**

Mark 13:12: **"Now the brother shall betray the brother to death, and the father the son; and children shall rise up against their parents and shall cause them to be put to death."**

- without distinction of sex to a child.

Titus 1:6: **"If any be blameless, the husband of one wife, having faithful children not accused of riot or unruly."**

- Posterity, seed

So often, with emphasis: to be regarded as genuine, true children,

Romans 9:7: **"nor are they all children because they are the seed of Abraham; but, "In Isaac your seed shall be called."**

B. τέκνα,

- Children brought into existence by **virtue of divine promise** (Romans 9:8); considered as children begotten by virtue of God's promise (Galatians 4:28), children by natural descent (Romans 9:8).

- In a broader sense (like Hebrew), Posterity (Matthew 2:18), with emphasis on true descent, true posterity (John 8:39); (of women) to be regarded as children (1 Peter 3:6). Specifically, a male child, a son (Matthew 21:28).

Jesus gives an illustration of heavenly and earthly fathers, one described as a wicked man who can nevertheless give good things to his children, and the other as a good father, saying: **"If ye then, being evil, know how to give good gifts unto your children, how much more shall your Father which is in heaven give good things to them that ask him?"** Matthew 7:11 (KJV).

Finally, the term "Huios".

We are now ready to look at the Huios stage of growth. This is the word in the Greek New Testament for 'son' of God, as in Romans 8:14. The defining characteristic of a son of God is that the Spirit leads them. Many Christians think they are at this 'son' level because they receive reve-lation, including and especially babies (Matthew 11:25). You must know your Father, actively seek your Lord, and have a strong 'handle' on sin in your life before you can be conside-red at this Huios level of growth.

The first thing Jesus said about 'sons of God' is that they are peacemakers (Matthew 5:9); not peaceful, or peacekeepers, but peacemakers. They go in and end fights. They love their enemies and pray for their persecutors (Matthew 5:45). They are completely matured, lacking no basic requirement of godliness (Matthew 5:48).

They are the good seed, the sons of the Kingdom (Matthew 13:38). They are to be separate from unbelievers, iniquity, darkness and idols (2 Corinthians 6:14-18). They are heirs of God (Galatians 4:7) and are brought to glory (Hebrews 2:10).

They do not sleep spiritually, but put on the armor of God, exhorting and building each other up (1 Thessalonians 5:5-11). They are offered up (James 2:21, Romans 12:1, Philippians 2:17). They learn obedience through suffering (Hebrews 5:8). They are chastened by the Lord (Hebrews 12:5). They are beloved of the Father (2 Peter 1:17). They are 'as He is' in this world, His perfect representatives (1 John 4:17).

They are led by the Spirit of God. This is their defining characteristic (Romans 8:14). When you see a Christian who says and does the right thing at the right time consistently, you can well assess that you are in the presence of a HUIOS level believer.

Another word in the Greek NT that is closely related to Huios is NEANISKOI. The NEANISKOI are the 'young men'. Perhaps this would be a category between the TEKNON and the HUIOS, because it would appear from Matthew 19:20 that NEANISKOI still lacks the 'perfection' of the HUIOS. But NEANISKOI see visions (Acts 2:17) and serve leadership (Acts 5:10). Young men are strong, the Word of God abides in them, and they have overcome the wicked one (1 John 2:13,14).

As we can see, God is deeply invested in the spiritual growth of every individual. Regardless of the stage of development one is in, the Father understands and meets each person where they are, providing what they need according to their level of maturity. He is the God of spiritual infants, those more advanced in their faith, and even mature sons who honor Him through the quality of their lives and the service they offer. Above all, the most important aspect is the establishment of a Father-son relationship, no matter the stage of development they may find themselves in.

Unfortunately, many struggle to experience the benefits of their relationship with God the Father because of bad experiences they have had with their earthly fathers. Understand that our heavenly Father will never take His love away from you.

2 Samuel 7:14 (KJV): **"I will be his father, and he shall be my son."**

This prayer is based on the bond of paternity between father and son. It is important to understand the significance of this relationship, to enjoy and benefit from the work of the Cross, by living victoriously.

PART II

MEN SHALL COME TO YOU

A man in Christ who deeply understands God's attributes, particularly His fatherhood and our sonship, will naturally pursue a deeper intimacy with Him throughout his earthly journey. For such a person, prayer becomes not just a routine practice but a meaningful and indispensable part of daily life, reflecting the desire to continually strengthen this divine relationship.

What does prayer mean to you? What are the benefits of prayer?

God's Word says that all men will come to Him. Prayer has different meanings for several reasons. The greatest power of prayer lies in its ability to sustain and nurture our communion with the Father.

Consequently, prayer is one of the strategic keys that defines our communion (Koinonia in Greek, rendered as communion in English) with the Father. It is one of the main tools for communion, alongside others, such as meditation.

1 Corinthians 1:9 (KJV): **"God is faithful, who has called you into fellowship with his Son, Jesus Christ our Lord."**

Communion: (Koinonia = sharing together - intimacy - relationship - participation). Anything that robs your communion robs your potential.

In fact, prayer is a command and a requirement: «Never stop praying.» 1 Thessalonians 5:17 (NLT).

Prayer is a means of change and transformation (Metamorpho).

"About eight days later Jesus took Peter, John, and James up on a mountain to pray. And as he was praying, the appearance of his face was transformed, and his clothes became dazzling white." Luke 9:28- 29 (NLT)

Prayer is a formidable weapon. Whenever a person prays, they become like an exposed electric wire; touching them can lead to harm. A believer who does not pray is vulnerable; it is only a matter of time before they face difficulties they cannot withstand. However, for a person of prayer, challenges can become opportunities for divine manifestation. Let us discipline ourselves to pray continually.

V.

UNDERSTANDING PRAYER

Prayer is an indispensable part of a believer's life in Christ. Those who grasp this truth will value and prioritize their prayer time, for the act of prayer is a form of spiritual governance over earthly matters; it is a time of creativity. Something profound occurs when we immerse ourselves in prayer.

Understanding and mastering these principles will firmly establish your prayer Ministry. Proverbs 24:3 (KJV): **"Through wisdom is an house builded; and by understanding it is established."**

Prayer is seen as a fruitful dialogue, an effective means of communication between us and the Lord, a platform through which God's kingdom and will are manifested on earth.

2 Chronicles 7:1-3 (ESV): **"As soon as Solomon finished his prayer, fire came down from heaven and consumed the burnt offering and the sacrifices, and**

the glory of the LORD filled the temple. And the priests could not enter the house of the LORD, because the glory of the LORD filled the LORD's house. When all the people of Israel saw the fire come down and the glory of the LORD on the temple, they bowed down with their faces to the ground on the pavement and worshiped and gave thanks to the LORD, saying, "For he is good, for his steadfast love endures forever."

From the very beginning, God's desire has always been to commune (Koinonia in Greek) with humankind, created in His image and likeness. From the very beginning of time, history records that when the Lord God created humanity, His voice would resound in the Garden of Eden every day in the cool of the evening, seeking communion with His creation.

The Apostle James, when reflecting on prayer, evoked the life of a great man of prayer, the prophet Elijah. He specifically pointed out that this was a man of the same nature as you and me, who was powerful in prayer and created opportunities.

The same apostle James was one of the twelve disciples who asked Jesus to teach them how to pray. What is shocking about this story is who these twelve disciples are. Aren't they Jews? They certainly used to attend the synagogue every Sabbath and knew all the rules of engagement according to the Law of Moses and their tradition. Yet they asked Jesus to bring them into the prayer academy. What does prayer mean to the Jews?

To understand just how essential prayer is for believers, let us first examine prayer in the context of the Jewish people.

For Jews, prayer consists of three main parts. Remember that Jesus' disciples were Jews and knew how to pray religiously. Surprisingly, one day they asked Jesus to teach them how to pray.

The word «prayer» comes from the Hebrew word "Tefilah". Experts agree that this is not an exact translation, as to pray means "to implore, beg or plead", for which we have a number of Hebrew words that translate this meaning more accurately. Whenever we turn to God in prayer, it must not be just to make requests, as if he is unaware of our needs.

Obviously, such a practice is acceptable and should be part of our conversation, but overall, our moments of prayer are much more than an attempt to get things from God. Psalms 69:13 (KJV): **«But as for me, my prayer is unto thee, O LORD, in an acceptable time: O God, in the multitude of thy mercy hear me, in the truth of thy salvation.»**

The interesting thing is that we cannot afford not to pray; God does not need our prayers; He actually can do without them. Therefore, one way of doing things right is to recognize the importance of our dependence on God in this world and in the hereafter.

God owes us nothing but gives us everything. We should also try to do the same for others and grant our favor freely. We should express our gratitude to God not only in words, but also in deeds: by obeying His sincere wishes to commandments and leading our daily lives as He wishes, even *more* so because it is for our own good.

Knowing that God is good and that nothings is impossible for Him, we can lead our lives with a deep sense of confidence and security. Even in times of distress, we will not despair, knowing that in some way (best known to God), everything that happens to us is for our good, a true blessing in disguise.

We do not like to suffer, so most of the time we pray to help us out of our distress and grant us the good that is neither hidden nor disguised, but the good that is manifestly evident, even to our fleshly eyes and limited understanding.

We gain strength, courage, and hope from our trust in God. Our daily prayers further strengthen our trust in Him.

A time for self-judgment

«The Hebrew word tefilah (הלפת) is derived from the verb pallel (ללפ), meaning 'to judge'. When we use the reflexive verb lehitpallel ('to pray'), it also carries the meaning of 'to judge oneself'. Therefore, prayer time is a period for self-judgment and self-assessment.»

When individuals approach God in prayer seeking His blessings, they must inevitably examine their hearts to assess whether they align with the standards of daily conduct set by God for humanity. Genuine self-reflection fosters humility, as individuals acknowledge their shortcomings and recognize that they scarcely merit the blessings and favors they request.

«Prayer empowers us to live fully according to God's intentions, enriching every aspect of our lives.»

Avodah - Service

The ultimate level of prayer reaches avodah, which means 'service'. The Old Testament (the Law of Moses) instructs the Children of Israel to serve God with all their heart. What type of service can truly be considered service of the heart? Prayer. In this context, prayer serves to purify both our nature and our heart.

The ordinary meaning of the word avodah is «work».

Consider a manufacturing plant: we begin with raw materials that undergo transformation into refined, finished products. Throughout this process, considerable time is spent removing waste or roughness from the raw materials, whether it is a rough diamond or a simple piece of wood, shaping them into objects of value or utility.

Tefilah, in the sense of avodah, is the «refining» process by which the impurities of man's character are eliminated. These unpleasant traits come from man's «animal» soul and are «natural» to him.

Nevertheless, humanity is endowed with a soul of divine nature, a reflection of God's own essence. This soul carries traces of divinity itself, encompassing all the noble attributes that set humans apart and elevate them above animals in their capacity and purpose. During our prayer sessions, our divine soul communicates with God, and even the animal soul is imbued with holiness. As a result, we feel cleansed and purified by this «service». When we return to our daily activities, the sense of holiness and purity remains, elevating our conduct throughout the day.

Tefilah - attachment

The most significant level of prayer is reached when we are inspired to the point of desiring nothing more than a deep sense of attachment to God. At this point, tefilah is related to the Hebrew verb «tofel», which means «to tie», «to join», or «to bind together», much like putting two pieces of a broken vase together to make it whole again.

In English, we have the word «enjoin», which means «to command», because a command serves as the link that unites the person being commanded with the one who commands, regardless of the distance, rank, or position that separates them.

When a supreme ruler orders a servant of the lowest rank to do something, it immediately establishes a bond between them. The servant feels honored that his master has noticed him and given him an assignment, allowing him, an individual of little or no influence, to perform a duty to please his superior. This eagerness motivates him to be worthy of his superior's favor and attention.

Indeed, our soul has been called "God's candle." Just as the flame of a candle constantly flickers, yearning to ascend and detach from its wick and the body of the candle, so too does our soul strive to rise. This is the very nature of fire—to move upward. Similarly, our soul inherently desires to ascend, reaching for the divine, whether we are consciously aware of it or not. Through prayer, we connect ourselves to God in a profound "spirit to spirit" bond. In this sacred act, our soul soars upwards, seeking to unite with God in a deeper communion.

Indeed, nothing brings man closer to God than prayer, which is truly the outpouring of the soul and therefore enables a «spirit-to-spirit attachment», as mentioned above. If we consider that every moment spent in prayer brings us closer to God, then prayer is like an embrace of God. It gives us a wonderful spiritual elevation and bliss, that there is no greater pleasure or satisfaction.

Yes, it is indeed remarkable that Jesus' disciples, who were Jews and deeply ingrained in their religious tradition, were astonished by the level of productivity demonstrated by Jesus Christ. He surpassed the typical expectations of what one man could achieve.

«How to pray? Why is prayer so vital in the life of the believer? Can you pray and get results?» Understand that life is spiritual and that prayer is essential and plays a key role in our walk with Him.

If we want to bring the invisible world into this earthly realm, we need to understand the mystery of prayer. «Blessed be the God and Father of our Lord Jesus Christ, who hath blessed us with all spiritual blessings in heavenly places in Christ.» Ephesians 1:3 (KJV)

Please, do not pray just because everyone else is praying or because you are told to pray. When you do not see immediate results, it is easy to become weary and discouraged, which can tarnish your prayer experience. But do not give up; prayer works. If it worked for our forefathers, it will work for us too and yield the desired results.

PRAY WITH PURPOSE AND INTENTION

Prayer is a profound spiritual mystery given to the saints, empowering them to exercise dominion over the world.

Until you grasp the significance of prayer within the divine framework, you will persist in your attempts to fulfill unfinished tasks, experience repeated failures, and struggle to achieve consistent results in life. In a parable, the Lord Jesus Christ illustrated how prayer is a potent mechanism of dominion. Remarkably, this truth remains profoundly relevant today.

The judge in this story showed no regard for God or man, yet the persistent widow kept going back to him, repeating her plea, and insisting that he deliver justice against her adversary. Initially indifferent to her plight, the unjust judge ignored her requests. Jesus then shared this parable with his disciples to teach them the importance of persistent prayer and not giving up.

In the book of Luke 18 1 -7 (NIV), He said: "In a certain town there was a judge who neither feared God nor cared what people thought. And there was a widow in that town who kept coming to him with the plea, 'Grant me justice against my adversary.' "For some time he refused. But finally he said to himself, 'Even though I don't fear God or care what people think, yet because this widow keeps bothering me, I will see that she gets justice, so that she won't eventually come and attack me!'" And the Lord said, "Listen to what the unjust judge says. And will not God bring about justice for his chosen ones, who cry out to him day and night? Will he keep putting them off?"

There is an important lesson to be learned from this story. We must be patient and persistent when we pray.

Just as the widow kept going back and pleading with the heartless judge, we should not give up easily. Through this parable, Jesus teaches the importance of perseverance in prayer. As the widow continued to insist and go back to the judge, he eventually granted her request because he grew weary of her persistence (Luke 18:5).

What a powerful revelation! Our perseverance can wear down even the greatest forces of darkness. In the book of Daniel, we witness Daniel's persistence in prayer for 21 days until the angel Gabriel arrives with the answer he sought. Gabriel reveals that the response had been dispatched from the very first day of his prayer, but was delayed by spiritual opposition (Daniel 10).

Similarly, in our own lives, the breakthrough we seek may come through our unwavering perseverance in prayer. By maintaining a consistent and fervent prayer life, we can wear down the enemy, forcing him to relent and release his grip on us.

Regardless of a person's weakness, perseverance in prayer can lead to significant breakthroughs, illuminating their path forward.

Through the power of language, individuals can actively shape a brighter future for themselves.

Listen to what Jesus said to his disciples in Matthew 17:20 (KJV): **"... for verily I say unto you, If ye have faith as a grain of mustard seed, ye shall say unto this mountain..."**

What a powerful message! The Lord Jesus emphasizes our responsibility as architects of our own destiny. Whatever we declare in prayer, confess with our lips, and truly believe in our hearts, we will witness the fulfillment of those petitions.

In biblical times, King Hezekiah was lying on a sickbed when he was visited by the prophet Isaiah and conveyed what the Lord had commanded him to do. He said : "The Lord of hosts has sent to tell you to put your house in order, for you are going to die."

Isaiah 38: 10 - 11, 17 – 20 (KJV): **"I said in the cutting off of my days, I shall go to the gates of the grave: I am deprived of the residue of my years. I said, I shall not see the LORD, even the LORD, in the land of the living: I shall behold man no more with the inhabitants of the world. ... Behold, for peace I had great bitterness: but thou hast in love to my soul delivered it from the pit of corruption: for thou hast cast all my sins behind thy back. For the grave cannot praise thee, death can not celebrate thee: they that go down into the pit cannot hope for thy truth. The living, the living, he shall praise thee, as I do this day: the father to the children shall**

make known thy truth. The LORD was ready to save me: therefore we will sing my songs to the stringed instruments all the days of our life in the house of the LORD."

He continued to speak to God in this way and to relay God's word. Here is what surprisingly happened: As the prophet was leaving the palace, God stopped him in the middle of the way and sent him back to the king. The Lord said to him: **"...Then came the word of the LORD to Isaiah, saying, Go, and say to Hezekiah, Thus saith the LORD, the God of David thy father, I have heard thy prayer, I have seen thy tears: behold, I will add unto thy days fifteen years."** Isaiah 38:4- 5 (KJV)

Stop looking around at your circumstances; instead, focus on God. Push yourself to overcome every obstacle by declaring and speaking words filled with conviction and power. When you do this, you will witness walls crumbling before you and seas parting right in front of you. Remember, prayer is one of the key spiritual platforms available to create the change we seek in our lives.

Prayer gives birth to ideas.

Prayer is particularly important in the life of the believer. If you really want to see God manifest Himself in your life, you must pray. As soon as you make up your mind to pray, something will happen. Unfortunately, many people do not know why or how they should talk to God.

If you need an idea, get down on your knees. Most of the time, it is through prayer that we receive spiritual enlightenment and grasp the reality we have been struggling to comprehend with our human minds; in an instant, we get a glimpse of it and begin to see.

I am not suggesting that revelations or insights are exclusive to prayer. For instance, in the Bible, Jacob received direction through a vision at night, and Joseph's guidance came without him specifically being in prayer. These examples show that God can provide revelation and orientation in various ways, not limited solely to moments of prayer.

Genesis 31:10-12 (ESV): **"In the breeding season of the flock I lifted up my eyes and saw in a dream that the goats that mated with the flock were striped, spotted, and mottled. Then the angel of God said to me in the dream, 'Jacob,' and I said, 'Here I am!' And he said, 'Lift up your eyes and see, all the goats that mate with the flock are striped, spotted, and mottled, for I have seen all that Laban is doing to you.'"**

Almighty God can speak to you through the creativity of your mind, bringing forth new ideas and insights. God has many ideas in store for you!

This is the key to accessing everything you want to see manifested in your life. Accessing God's ideas is vital for Christians as they navigate their earthly journey.

BECOME PASSIONATE AND ENTHUSIASTIC

It is time to rekindle your prayer life. Jesus Christ led the way; he was admired by the Jews for achieving great results from his prayer life. The prayer life of many men and women of God we admire and desire to imitate, is more often the expression of a long journey of faith, commitment, and dedication. Remember that results do not appear overnight; in fact, they are the crowning achievement of a commitment to pray again and again.

To prepare for the harvest season, farmers must carefully follow essential steps and meet all necessary requirements, ensuring a successful farming season and the enjoyment of a bountiful harvest.

This revelation has impacted my personal prayer life, and ignited a greater hunger for worship, praise, and solitary celebration in my prayer closet. I became eager to explore what motivated and empowered these spiritual leaders to become impactful individuals through prayer and how they could achieve so much. What was the secret behind their success?

When one carefully reads and studies David's psalms, they realize the depth and passion behind his words. That is why I decided to explore the prayer lives of other successful people, to understand how their commitment and dedication to prayer, along with their trust in God, led to positive outcomes. These heroes of faith serve as inspirations, and prove how prayers made in Jesus' name are heard and answered by our heavenly Father.

I realized that the power of a praying individual and its impact, lies in the combination of faith in God's word, prayer, and unwavering belief. These individuals understand the trustworthiness of God's promises. By firmly believing in His word and maintaining a consistent prayer life, they have experienced the fulfillment of their petitions.

It is truly astounding how ministers of past generations achieved so much and reached so many people, even in remote areas. They were called to travel great distances from their home countries to spread the gospel around the world. A key secret to their success was their unwavering dedication and devotion to a consistent prayer life, and faith in the word of the living God, knowing that He rewards those who earnestly seek Him. Figures such as Elijah, Hezekiah, Moses, and Joshua are just a few examples of individuals who exemplified a life of prayer.

For example, Hudson Taylor's approach to prayer and preparation for his mission in China serves as a powerful example. His trust in God and his discipline of remaining silent after prayer, fully relying on the Lord, can deeply impact and inspire others. His life reminds us of the importance of trusting in God's plans, even when faced with uncertainty. His example is a valuable lesson on the power of steadfast faith and prayer.

In the midst of life's challenges and impossibilities, a prayer of faith, made with deep conviction based on the Word of the living God and inspired by the Holy Spirit, will yield great results at the time set by God's counsel, no matter the circumstances or how long it may take. «**Men ought always to pray, and not to faint."** Luke 18:1 (KJV)

Why do men pray? The answer to this question is manifold. Indeed, men approach God in prayer for several reasons. They ask, intercede, praise, and adore Him in various situations. No wonder the apostle James says: "Is anyone among you in trouble? Let him pray." James 5:13 (KJV). However, notice what the Bible says: "Men ought always to pray, and not to faint."

There are several compelling reasons why a Christian needs to pray. While prayer is a common practice in many religious traditions, this book specifically focuses on the prayer of a believer—one who prays to God (his Father, referred to as "Abba" in Hebrew) in the name of Jesus Christ. **"This is how you should pray: "After this manner therefore pray ye: Our Father which art in heaven, Hallowed be thy name. Thy kingdom come. Thy will be done in earth, as it is in heaven. Give us this day our daily bread.**

And forgive us our debts, as we forgive our debtors. And lead us not into temptation, but deliver us from evil." Matthew 6:9-13 (KJV)

From a biblical perspective, prayer can be defined as a devout request to God or an object of worship; it involves spiritual communion, supplication, thanksgiving, adoration, or confession. It implies being proactive :

1. Intentionally setting time aside for prayer. We learn to pray by spending time alone in prayer, as instructed by Jesus in Matthew 6:6, "But when you pray, go into your room and shut the door and pray to your Father who is in secret." On the other hand, we can also set aside time to pray together with others.

2. Your desire to pray increases as you engage in collective prayer experiences. A time when the emphasis is on prayer, a session where scriptural principles of prayer are emphasized and applied.

3. Meditating on the men and women of prayer in the Bible, such as Elijah, Hezekiah, David, or our Lord Jesus.

4. By reading books about the prayers of God's generals who walked in victory, by associating prayer with their daily walk and their relationship with the Creator.

5. Teaching that is selective and rooted in God's word, delivered by God-fearing individuals, can be multiplied more effectively as the Holy Spirit guides, leads, and counsels us in all things.

VI.

PRAYER IN THE LIFE OF A BELIEVER

Your prayers are important.

Prayer is the essence and core of Christian life, as well as of many other religions. In today's world, however, philosophy often undermines the power of praying to God for His intervention in the affairs of mankind. Yuval N. H, best-selling author, once said: «Generation after generation, humans have prayed to God to intervene in their affairs.»

Despite generations praying to various gods, angels, and saints, and creating countless tools, institutions, and social systems, humanity has continued to suffer from famine, pandemics, and violence, with millions perishing.

Many thinkers and prophets have concluded that famine, pestilence, and war are either part of God's cosmic plan or a result of our imperfect nature, and that only the end of time could free us from these afflictions.

"We don't need to pray to a god or a saint to deliver us from them." This quote highlights the extent to which prayer is increasingly underestimated and misunderstood by many. Note that as Christians, we do not pray to angels or saints. Our prayers are directed to our heavenly Father, God, in the name of Jesus.

When people do not achieve expected results after praying or when things do not go as planned, it is not because of God's shortcomings.

More often, it is due to a lack of understanding of the prayer principles that lead to results. The prophet Hosea provides a powerful key: whenever something goes wrong in our lives, the issue typically lies with us, not with God.

Haggai 1:6-7 (KJV): **"Ye have sown much, and bring in little; ye eat, but ye have not enough; ye drink, but ye are not filled with drink; ye clothe you, but there is none warm; and he that earneth wages earneth wages to put it into a bag with holes. Thus, saith the LORD of hosts; Consider your ways."**

If our prayers have not yielded results in the past, it is most likely because we lack a fundamental understanding of prayer. Prayer serves as the bedrock of our Christian life. Eternal life, fellowship, and the Scriptures, hold little value if we neglect prayer. Through prayer, we engage our spirits to access the provision within us. In fact, everything we require for life resides within, but without prayer, we fail to unlock God's blessings.

Prayer is a weapon for these end times. It is like a weapon of mass destruction. In fact, a Christian on his knees is as powerful as an atomic bomb. His prayer can affect any situation and damage the enemy's camp; even James said that prayer availeth much (James 5:16 AMP).

Let us examine the case of Elijah and what happened when he confronted the prophets of Baal. After challenging them to invoke their god, Elijah proceeded to rearrange the altar, place the sacrifice upon it, and pour water over it. Then, he called upon the name of the Lord, and suddenly, fire came down from heaven, consuming the entire offering.

1Kings 18: 29-40: **"And as midday passed, they raved on until the time of the offering of the oblation, but there was no voice. No one answered, no one paid attention. Then Elijah said to all the people, "Come near to me." And all the people came near to him. And he repaired the altar of the Lord that had been thrown down. Elijah took twelve stones, according to the number of the tribes of the sons of Jacob, to whom the word of the Lord came, saying, "Israel shall be your name," and with the stones he built an altar in the name of the Lord. And he made a trench about the altar, as great as would contain two seahs[a] of seed. And he put the wood in order and cut the bull in pieces and laid it on the wood. And he said, "Fill four jars with water and pour it on the burnt offering and on the wood."**

And he said, "Do it a second time." And they did it a second time. And he said, "Do it a third time." And they did it a third time. And the water ran around the altar and filled the trench also with water. And at the time of the offering of the oblation, Elijah the prophet came near and said, "O Lord, God of Abraham, Isaac, and Israel, let it be known this day that you are God in Israel, and that I am your servant, and that I have done all these things at your word. Answer me, O Lord, answer me, that this people may know that you, O Lord, are God, and that you have turned their hearts back." Then the fire of the Lord fell and consumed the burnt offering and the wood and the stones and the dust, and licked up the water that was in the trench. And when all the people saw it, they fell on their faces and said, "The Lord, he is God; the Lord, he is God."

Prayer is a great tool for spiritual **transformation**.

Luke 9:29-31 (KJV): **"As he was praying, the appearance of his face changed, and his clothes became as bright as a flash of lightning. 30 Two men, Moses and Elijah, appeared in glorious splendor, talking with Jesus. 31 They spoke about his departure, which he was about to bring to fulfillment at Jerusalem."**

Moses went up to the mountain for forty days and forty nights; when he came down with the two tablets of the covenant, he did not realize his face was shining brightly because he had been talking with God (Exodus 34:29-35). The more time you spend with God in prayer, the more you are strengthened, changed, and empowered to face the challenges of life and continue your walk of faith with the help of the Holy Spirit. Make no mistake about it : a believer who does not pray will be a victim of circumstances.

Prayer was a lifestyle of our forefathers. No wonder these men and women of faith won great battles and were established in positions of influence (Hebrews 11:1-2).

The Bible provides examples of the prayer lives of men and women of God who distinguished themselves in this spiritual discipline, becoming benchmarks for generations to come. Their legacy of faith and prayer speaks for itself.

King David is one of the notable examples of a believer who developed intimacy with God through prayer.

The prophet Elijah's style of prayer reveals profound truths about a powerful servant of God who distinguished himself in this spiritual discipline (James 5:17). In fact, James enthusiastically highlights Elijah's approach to prayer, offering a remarkable presentation on the subject in the fifth chapter of his epistle.

Every time I am inspired to pray, I feel enthusiastic and confident. I know these moments of prayer are exceptional and cannot be replaced by anything else. That is when earth is connected to heaven. Indeed, we connect with our heavenly father through the medium of prayer.

That is why it is so important for every Christian, wherever they are, to understand the importance of prayer. Through our prayers, we influence the course of our lives, our families, our communities, and the world. A life without prayer for believers is like spiritual suicide for the world.

Can you imagine our world without altars of prayer? In a world filled with all kinds of evils, **"Days are evil, walk carefully."** (Ephesians 5:14,16-17).

I am convinced that one of the many ways to walk carefully is to develop and maintain a quality prayer life. Tragedies happen every day, wars break out without warning, famines appear overnight, and diseases keep on spreading by surprise. Moments of prayer are moments of creativity, when heaven and earth collide. The Bible affirms that God is on His throne and that men must always pray and not falter (Luke 18).

Prayer is a key that can unlock the manifestation of the mystery of God's kingdom on earth and bring heaven to earth. **"Thy kingdom come on earth as it is in heaven."** (Matthew 6:10)

When we pray the right way, heavenly doors open, and God's glory manifests in our circumstances.

One of the most fascinating studies on prayer is found in the book of James, which I highly recommend to all devoted Christians. I am particularly amazed by how James references the righteous man in prayer, pointing to the prophet Elijah as an example.

He says: **"Elijah, a man of the same nature as ourselves, prayed."** (James 5:17)

Another story is that of the disciples. One day they saw Jesus praying and noticed he was getting results, so they stopped him and asked: "Master, teach us to pray." (Luke 11:1-4)

VII.

PRAYER MAKES POWER AVAILABLE

No believer can live a victorious Christian life without the power of the Holy Spirit. Jesus Christ mentioned that he had much to pass on to his disciples, but they did not yet have the capacity to carry it (John 16:12). He later clarified that when they receive the Holy Spirit, they will be able to accomplish much more. The apostle speaks of God who can do, through the power that acts in us, infinitely beyond our thoughts and our imagination (Ephesians 3:20).

The Holy Spirit intervenes in our moments of prayer and prays for us (Romans 8:26).

To live a life of consistent prayer, we must understand how to operate in the power of the Holy Spirit.

Jesus told his disciples in Acts 1:8 (KJV): **"You shall receive power…"**

According to the apostle James (James 1:16-17), we make extraordinary power available to us when we pray.

First, we must understand what power is and then act with diligence in prayer. The word 'power' is translated from the Greek as:

1. **Exousia** - (The authority we acquire through our position in Christ).

We are seated in heavenly places at the right hand of His Majesty. It is similar to the uniform of a police officer on duty. Just by seeing the uniform, we immediately recognize who they are and acknowledge the authority they carry.

Matthew 10:1 (KJV): **"And when he had called unto him his twelve disciples, he gave them power against unclean spirits, to cast them out, and to heal all manner of sickness and all manner of disease."**

2. **Dunamis** - (Dynamos, like a generator producing effects, electricity). This type of power is obtained through prayer and declaration.

Acts 1:8 (KJV): **"But ye shall receive power, after that the Holy Ghost is come upon you: and ye shall be witnesses unto me both in Jerusalem, and in all Judaea, and in Samaria, and unto the uttermost part of the earth."**

3. **Anagkazo** - irresistible power

Luke 14:23 (KJV): **"…Go out into the highways and hedges, and compel [anagkazo] them to come in, that my house may be filled."**

God's power comes upon you, and His presence dwells within you permanently. The Holy Spirit's presence is a dormant power within you. If you choose to activate it, you will witness remarkable results.

The book of Corinthians talks about the gifts of the Spirit. One of them is the gift of tongues (speech, prayer, or interpretation, as seen in 1 Corinthians 12:14). The Apostle Paul clearly demonstrated the place of this gift. His teaching on tongues is amazing. First, **"I pray in tongues, then in understanding."** He who speaks in tongues speaks mysteries and speaks to God. He edifies himself. The word «edify» here means he builds himself up (1 Corinthians 14:4).

When you pray in tongues, power is released. What you do with this power will determine the course of your life. If you do not take advantage of that power, your life will not change much, even if power is released for you. Power must be used for the purpose of doing something. Many Christians have not known this secret I am sharing.

They spend good times praying in tongues, stirring up so much power, but then they walk away without saying a word. Thank God for speaking in tongues. But it is not enough. When you pray in tongues, after a while, tremendous power will be released; you will know it when it happens - you will be overcome with strong power. At that point, you need to take advantage of the released power and use it however you want.

I remember a time several years ago when I faced a rent issue. I had accumulated more than six months' worth of arrears, and for many months, I didn't have a permanent job.

The landlord trusted us and barely checked his bank account. I do not know what happened that day, but for the very first time we stayed in his apartment, he decided to check our payment history and noticed we had been late for several months. He could not believe it as he trusted us. As he decided to pay us a visit in the middle of the night, he heard someone praying with heavy, deep, mighty tongues for an uncommonly long time. He left and came back the next day.

He decided to visit our apartment in the evening and met my beautiful wife. He then asked her why we had not paid the rent for so many months. "My husband does not have a steady job", my wife replied. "Why didn't you tell me? I trusted you!" said the landlord. "When I checked my account and realized that the money was missing, I thought you were like everybody else. But I was surprised when I came last night; I heard your husband praying in tongues; I understood that this man was a servant of God", he said.

Then my wife told him what we have been going through for the past few months.

You can maximize your prayer potential with the help of the Holy Spirit. Praying in tongues was part of my breakthrough process. By praying in tongues, I spoke mysteries into being while I was in trouble, and the Holy Spirit used the circumstances to glorify God. Hallelujah.

The man was electrified by the power of the Holy Spirit through my speaking in tongues. He went to the ATM, withdrew money, and handed my wife a generous sum of money, enough to cover our household expenses for two months. This sum was non-refundable. What a miracle! How do you explain this scenario? The person to whom I owed a generous amount of money became a great financial blessing to my family.

Your prayer can change decisions and favor you every time you find yourself in a difficult situation. If you choose to pray, you will unleash tremendous power in operation.

Eventually, I secured a high-paying expatriate job with great benefits, and God transformed our finances to such an extent that we became partners in the TV ministry, the healing school, and the Inner-City Mission of the church I served in.

Praying in tongues as much as possible will keep you out of trouble. It is another form of spiritual high-tech language that accelerates spiritual realities. Please understand that you can express your well-being through speaking in tongues.

1 Corinthians 14:2 (KJV): **"For he that speaketh in an unknown tongue speaketh not unto men, but unto God: for no man understandeth him; howbeit in the spirit he speaketh mysteries."**

Affirmation after a time of communion with the Holy Spirit.

One time, as I was looking for a new job, I took some days for prayer and fasting. I recall that on the last day of this small retreat, something happened that changed my prayer life. In fact, I cannot tell how many hours I spent in God's presence because I was soaked in prayer. As I was praying in tongues for an exceptionally lengthy period, I suddenly heard a voice whispering into my ears: "What the heavens has granted, the earth cannot take it away." Suddenly, the tongues stopped immediately, and I knew I had just received the substance that I was looking for.

I started to confess audibly: "What the heavens have granted nobody can get from me." I went on and on, professing my faith for days until the right opportunity came my way, I took it with ease because I already had a sound of victory in my spirit. Glory be to God! The result came as I made the decision to trust God's word and the leading of the Holy

Spirit. The Gospel is trustworthy, and we can rely on it and get tangible results. No wonder the apostle Paul wrote in the book of Acts 20:32 (NIV): "Now, I commit you to God and to the word of his grace, which can build you up and give you an inheritance among all those who are sanctified."

The word "build" here refers to construction, suggesting the contribution of various elements in the process of creating a physical structure. In other words, the apostle is explaining that your life is like a spiritual building, requiring input at every stage for its progressive and qualitative construction. This process shapes you into God's final, indestructible creation, strong in His sight.

The knowledge of God's word will give you arguments in prayer. By praying with your understanding, you can place the right word from the Bible to center the attack and destroy the unfavorable realities that challenge you.

Stay under the guidance of the Holy Spirit by following His instructions.

John 16: 12 – 13 (NIV): **"I have much more to say to you, more than you can now bear. But when he, the Spirit of truth, comes, he will guide you into all the truth. He will not speak on his own; he will speak only what he hears, and he will tell you what is yet to come."**

Understand that the Holy Spirit lives within you and guides you. Follow His guidance even if you have no idea

what He's planning to do. You are the vehicle of His Shekinah, and He's the one behind the wheel. He can turn right,
left, or even go straight on without asking for your input. Yet,
do not forget that the vehicle, as a body, must be of service
to keep on welcoming the Father's mighty presence, for the
purpose of doing His will and desires on earth.

VIII.

DEVOTE YOURSELF TO PRAYER AND NEVER GIVE UP

The days are evil, and the times are hard. Stay strong and be intentional and determined in prayer. You do not have to wait for church prayer sessions; instead, build your own prayer altar as a priority. Exercise your prayer skills by structuring your prayer times for better results. You can achieve more on your knees, and when you show up in prayer, you make things happen.

The apostle Paul uses the term «devotion,» which comes from the Greek word (skholadzô [verb]; from skholê: entertainment).

1. **To give oneself over to**, to occupy oneself with something

«Defraud ye not one the other, except it be with consent for a time, that ye may give yourselves to fasting and prayer;». 1 Corinthians 7:5 (KJV).

2. **Diligent:** (éuparédros [adj. used as a noun]; from éu: good, para: in addition, and hédra: seat).

Paul was speaking to the Corinthians with a view to what is proper, and that they might attend (lit.: and diligently) to the Lord's service without distraction.

1 Corinthians 7:35 (KJV): **"And this I speak for your own profit; not that I may cast a snare upon you, but for that which is comely, and that ye may attend upon the Lord without distraction."**

I remember praying for a man many years ago, who had come to attend a healing school in Toronto but could not be accommodated during the session. My wife took him home and prayed for him.

Ingredients of this answered prayer:

1. The desire of the man who had lost his sight.

2. The faith we had in God for healing and miracles.

3. Our prayer produced tremendous power over time and produced a miracle. Today, the said man sees correctly.

For many years, I did not realize the power I could release through prayer.

James 5:14-15 says: **"He who prays gets results."** In other words, there are benefits associated with our commitment to prayer.

Stop quarreling; start praying. Stop complaining; start praying.

Stop blaming others for your failures; pray. Stop criticizing; start praying.

Understand that "A Christian on his knees is more powerful than any atomic bomb", as John Hagin once said.

When you are on your knees, talking to your heavenly Father in faith and believing that whatever you ask for, you'll receive, you're like a soldier on the front line wielding a weapon of mass destruction—the most powerful and destructive weapon that no enemy can resist.

The soldier knows why he is in the army, and what he wears allows him to exercise his authority. He remains confident and focused on victory, using the weapons at his disposal.

Another personal experience

I was relying on God to find a new job, then I came across a wonderful opportunity whose recruitment process was quite lengthy. I had to go through many interview stages and wait for months before being interviewed. Throughout the process, I prayed constantly. Finally, I signed my contract, started working, and the rest is history.

Consistency is observed in the prayer life of Jesus. Every morning while it was still dark, long before daylight appeared, he retired to a deserted place to pray (Mark 1: 35).

This book is not a doctrinal book; I am not talking about the doctrine of prayer, but rather the result you get when you apply God's principles regarding prayer, and when you obey. Do you pray? Show me the results of your prayers. Prayer in Jesus' name works if you follow the application of God's principles regarding prayer and obey and incline to the Holy Spirit's guidance. Hallelujah!

You can change your life and effect change in your community, business, and ministry through the ministry of prayer. As Apostle Joshua Selman once said : "Every moment is a time for prayer.» Pray without ceasing, do not slacken, and do not give up.

NEVER FALTER, NEVER DOUBT

Abraham's journey to beget Isaac indeed illustrates this truth. Sometimes when God speaks, it may not make sense to us immediately. It might take days, months, or even years for us to understand what God is about to do with us and through us.

Genesis 18:10 (NIV): **"Then one of them said, "I will surely return to you about this time next year, and Sarah your wife will have a son."**

I am trying to describe Abraham and Sarah's reactions. They both said, "Wonders never cease." That is what they were saying when God told them they would have their own child «this time next year» (Genesis 17:15-16, 19-21; 18:10, 13-14).

Can I pray and receive an answer within a specific time frame? It took Abraham a good 25 years before the promise became reality. A child was born to him and Sarah; they named him Isaac, which means 'smile'.

Anything you want to have under the sun can become yours as soon as you master the secrets or principles that govern and influence the physical world. Understand that what is seen proceeds from the invisible (the unseen).

Hebrew 11:3 (KJV): **"Through faith we understand that the worlds were framed by the word of God, so that things which are seen were not made of things which do appear."**

Job 38:33 (KJV): **"Knowest thou the ordinances of heaven? canst thou set the dominion thereof in the earth?"**

Prayer is seen as one of the platforms we can use to activate answers and live victoriously every day of our lives. Daniel read in the book that 70 years had to pass before Israel would come out of captivity, so he fasted and prayed for 21 days (Daniel 9:2).

Daniel's prayer functioned as the trigger for a gun, propelling the bullet of events into motion. What is intriguing is that Daniel prayed for 21 days before the angel Gabriel appeared. During this time, Gabriel disclosed some of the mysteries surrounding the interval between Daniel's prayer and their encounter. The Prince of Persia opposed him (Daniel 10:12). Daniel was unaware of the conflict unfolding in the unseen realm—a battle between light and darkness.

This type of prayer requires faith.

If you believe, you can command that mountain to move, and that is a prayer with divine timing.

Consider the woman with the issue of blood, as described in Luke 8:43-48. After suffering from her condition for twelve long years, she made a firm decision and set a time for her healing. What activated the healing power was "HER FAITH."

While many people may have touched the Lord Jesus, the distinction between their touches and the woman's was her insistence on receiving the grace available at that very moment. When Jesus felt power leave Him and inquired "Who touched me?", the woman, filled with fear, confessed. In response, Jesus said to her, "Daughter, be of good comfort: your faith has made you whole; go in peace."

The woman's decision was indeed courageous. It takes courage and determination to trust God in all things. Her prayer could have been : "Father God, I pray today that I will draw near to your servant, knowing you will release a blessing upon me. I will strive to reach him." However, she did not choose this path.

You can take a cue from this wonderful woman of faith. Through your moment of prayer, you can call upon God in Jesus' name and redirect Him for your own good. If only you understood how vital your role is in your own survival, you would not continue complaining and waiting; instead, you would make decisions right now. Like the woman with the issue of blood, who was astonished when Jesus noticed that virtue had left him. Engage in prayer today and witness the results you desire. Direct that power towards the determination in your heart, and you will undoubtedly see the results your faith will produce in prayer.

Timely prayer, coupled with strong conviction, will inevitably yield fruits. As you read this passage, harness your ability to pray and alter your circumstances.

I challenge you to step into Jesus' Kingdom Miracle store and exercise your faith by praying for a situation that has been dragging in your life for so long.

Regarding timely answers, I recall a significant delay I experienced while living in South Africa, awaiting for a work permit. I reached out to an immigration officer who was assisting me with the process. Without the necessary funds, I turned to prayer, trusting in God's provision. I believed that before the end of that year, I would have enough money to cover the permit expenses.

Before that, I attempted to reach out to a few friends, but to no avail. Therefore, I chose to remain calm and put my trust in the Lord.

Later that year, in December, my wonderful wife asked me, "Do you still believe in God for a breakthrough?" Without hesitation, I replied: "I do. God knows; prayer never fails."

As Christmas drew nearer, she approached me again, asking: "Do you still believe in God for a breakthrough?" She could see me seeking help from others without success.

Then, on the morning of December 31st, she posed the same question once more. And yet again, I gave her the same unwavering answer.

She returned later that day, around 10 pm on December 31st, with the same question. I remained composed and replied, "I believe in God in this situation, and prayer never fails."

We proceeded to church and engaged in prayer throughout the night. My phone remained in my pocket as I praised God for the blessings of the past year and for His wonders. Despite not receiving any news by midnight on the 31st, I persisted in prayer.

As the praise and worship continued and the midnight hour passed, the pastor proclaimed the arrival of the new year, and we exchanged hugs and heartfelt well wishes. Suddenly, I retrieved my phone and noticed several missed calls from before December 31st of that year, including one just minutes before; it was from my father-in-law.

I returned his call and we exchanged New Year wishes. He then mentioned: "Actually, I called you over an hour ago but couldn't reach you. I am calling now because I have earmarked a portion of my annual bonus for you. Please provide me with the necessary details so I can transfer the funds to you."

I was utterly astounded. Remembering how I had repeatedly affirmed my trust in God, declaring that prayer never fails, and expressing my belief in a miracle, all while hoping for the money by midnight on December 31st.

I received my answer just in time. Although it arrived on the second of the following year, just minutes before the end of the year, the money was just enough to cover the cost of my work permit.

Since adopting the mindset of «prayerful awareness», I have come to understand that God expects me to make requests and trust that He will answer, granting my heart's desires. It's no longer a surprise to me to witness individuals return from a service with testimonies of deliverance from various infirmities and experiencing newfound financial freedom.

Many have testified to remarkable healings, such as being cured of high blood pressure, skin diseases, and over a decade of back pain, as well as experiencing restored sight and hearing. Some have been resuscitated in emergency rooms, relieved of abdominal pain, and even had their debts paid off by divine intervention after years. Others have received scholarships, been healed of disorders without surgery, and encountered numerous other miracles. These experiences are tangible proof that God is real, and that prayer indeed works.

Jonah 2:7 (KJV): **"When my soul fainted within me I remembered the LORD: and my prayer came in unto thee, into thine holy temple."**

Colossians 4:2 (AMP) **: "Be persistent and devoted to prayer, being alert and focused in your prayer life with an attitude of thanksgiving."**

Continue steadfastly, be earnest, and remain tireless in prayer. Keep persevering and persisting in your prayers.

Luke 11:8 (KJV): **"I say unto you, Though he will not rise and give him, because he is his friend, yet because of his importunity he will rise and give him as many as he needeth."**

If we persist and pray as instructed in Luke 11:8, He will provide us with everything we need. Let us shift our mindset towards prayer. Let us not abandon prayer hastily. The Lord values our prayers. If only we grasp that He is eager to listen and delights in our conversation, we will approach every moment of prayer with seriousness and reverence.

Prayer is a mystery, which transcends ages and generations. It goes beyond your present circumstances and time. When you feel overwhelmed or under pressure, turn to prayer. It is in seeking more of God through prayer that we find solace and strength.

So, pray.

When you are feeling discouraged or stuck, unable to move forward, turn to prayer. Prayer has the power to uplift your spirit and provide guidance in times of uncertainty. So, in moments of discouragement or stagnation, pray.

It is time for you to rise in prayer and stand firm. Prayer enables you to elevate to new levels and undergo personal transformation.

Prayer unleashes tremendous power and dynamic in its operation. Through prayer, power becomes available—for change, for growth, for acceleration, and for anointing. The more you dedicate yourself to prayer, following biblical principles, the more impactful and effective your prayer life will become.

Prayer sessions are moments of revelation and creation. Personally, I would choose to spend six hours engaged in prayer—talking and listening to God—over driving for the same duration without uttering a word.

Today, I encourage you to pray and unleash the power generated during your prayer sessions to make a tangible impact.

Consider Moses, who spent forty days and nights in God's presence to receive the law. Similarly, Daniel fasted and prayed for 21 days to receive heaven's answer. When you devote time to prayer, you will witness the glory of God and have the privilege to glorify His holy name.

'"Moses said, "Please show me your glory." And he said, "I will make all my goodness pass before you and will proclaim before you my name 'The LORD..." Exodus 33:18-19 (KJV)

Invest as much time as you can in prayer, and you will unlock your prayer potential, bringing about significant outcomes.

Prayer is a formidable weapon; keep your faith strong and your focus on God as you pray, ensuring that you maintain momentum in your spiritual journey.

PART III

PRAY AND CREATE POSSIBILITIES

The Word of God unveils His wonderful plans for your life. With the guidance and assistance of the Holy Spirit, you can trust in the fulfillment of His promises and step into the boundless possibilities He offers through prayer.

Jeremiah 29,11 (NIV) : **"I know the plans that I have for you, plans to prosper you and not harm you."**

Understand that He is capable of far more than you can ever imagine or conceive.

Ephesians 3:20-21 (KJV): **"Now unto him that is able to do exceedingly abundantly above all that we ask or think, according to the power that worketh in us, unto him be glory in the church by Christ Jesus throughout all ages, world without end. Amen."**

All you have to do is tap into the vast reservoir of His grace through prayer, opening the door to limitless possibilities, for nothing is impossible with Him.

IX.

SPEAK AND MOVE MOUNTAINS

When you start praying, something marvelous will unfold in your life— your divine dimension will be stirred into action.

If we consider the life of the Apostle Paul, can we explain how the destiny of a murderer and the destiny of an apostle can be reconciled? How is this possible? How do these two elements come together?

My pastor shared with me the story of his conversion. He recounted how, one day, while his mother was attending a prayer meeting at a certain church, she received a message about her son's destiny. Despite her faithful prayers over many years, nothing seemed to change. Instead, the condition of her eldest son, mentioned in the prophecy, worsened.

The pastor revealed that he often returned home late and intoxicated. Despite this, his mother never ceased praying. He recalled catching glimpses of his mother on her knees, fervently praying: "God, change my son." His response would be: "Save your son from what?" Yet, she persevered, with an unwavering faith, clinging to God's word with all her heart, until her prayers were answered.

Prayer remains steadfast, even if years have passed by between the release of the word and its fulfillment. Eventually, her son surrendered his life to Christ and became a shepherd.

Prayer serves to open the atmosphere of heaven, acting as a gateway that unlocks the dimensions of the heavens. Through prayer, one can peer into the realm from which they originated, defining themselves from an eternal perspective rather than being constrained by time (Chronos).

Abraham was indeed wealthy in cattle, but his destiny surpassed mere material wealth. In a divine encounter, God instructed him to leave his homeland and depart from his birthplace, including his biological family.

Addressing Abraham, God questioned: "Who told you that your destiny is determined by the size of your herd and the abundance of your cattle? You are destined to become the father of a multitude of nations. Your identity extends far beyond being a mere owner of cattle; you are the patriarch of a multitude."

Suppose Abraham had never experienced that divine encounter; he might have defined himself solely by his material wealth, considering himself the wealthiest man of his time based on the abundance of his cattle. However, such a perspective would have been earthly and severely limited, failing to grasp the grandeur of God's plan for him.

Abraham, however, embarked on a journey that led him to the pinnacle of his life. Through his encounter with unseen destiny, he discovered that in God's dimension, possibilities are boundless. This realization stems from the fact that God created us in His own image and likeness.

To comprehend the mysteries of what lies ahead, we must undergo a multifaceted process of transformation:

1. **Mortification:** Your flesh will be subdued, allowing for spiritual growth and alignment with God's will.

2. **Renewal of the spirit:** You will be enlightened beyond the physical realm, transcending mere philosophy, and gaining deeper insights into spiritual truths.

Something remarkable occurs as we engage in prayer. The Apostle Paul references it in the eighteenth verse of the second chapter of his epistle to the Ephesians, describing it as «the eyes of our understanding» being enlightened. Through prayer, these spiritual eyes are opened, allowing us to perceive truths beyond the physical realm.

It is crucial to recognize that there exists another kind of sight—the «eyes of our understanding»—which grants us insight into realities beyond our immediate perception. These eyes of understanding offer us hope in our divine calling and illuminate the path before us.

These are riches that often go unheard of—treasures possessed by the saints, enlightening them with divine wisdom and understanding.

Ephesians 1:18 (KJV): **"The eyes of your understanding being enlightened; that ye may know what is the hope of his calling, and what the riches of the glory of his inheritance in the saints."**

The Master also mentioned for His disciples in Luke 24:45 (KJV): **"Then opened he their understanding, that they might understand the scriptures…"**

It is about connecting with a Power, but not just any power—it is the Power that raised Jesus from the dead. Only then can humanity begin to comprehend the essence of resurrection. As we become aware of these spiritual realities and the wealth we possess, everything we touch is infused with life. Even a failing company, when touched with spiritual understanding, can experience revival. While others see crisis, we perceive opportunity, leaving them wondering about our insight, unaware that «the eyes of our understanding are enlightened.

Comparing the destiny of a prostitute with that of Jesus Christ may seem like contrasting two vastly different worlds. However, through the lens of spiritual understanding, we recognize that both represent profound transformations. Just as Jesus' life exemplifies divine redemption and restoration, so too can the life of a repentant individual, regardless of their past, be transformed into one of redemption and purpose.

King Hezekiah overcame the threats of King Sennacherib of Syria and his words of defiance against the living God.

"After Hezekiah received the letter from the messengers and read it, he went up to the LORD's Temple and spread it out before the LORD. And Hezekiah prayed this prayer before the LORD: "O LORD of Heaven's Armies, God of Israel, you are enthroned between the mighty cherubim! You alone are God of all the kingdoms of the earth. You alone created the heavens and the earth. Bend down, O LORD, and listen! Open your eyes, O LORD, and see! Listen to Sennacherib's words of defiance against the living God. "It is true, LORD, that the kings of Assyria have destroyed all these nations.

And they have thrown the gods of these nations into the fire and burned them. But of course the Assyrians could destroy them! They were not gods at all— only idols of wood and stone shaped by human hands. Now, O LORD our God, rescue us from his power; then all the kingdoms of the earth will know that you alone, O LORD, are God. Then Isaiah son of Amoz sent this

message to Hezekiah: "This is what the LORD, the God of Israel, says: Because you prayed about King Sennacherib of Assyria." Isaiah 37:14-21 (NLT)

PRAYER WILL ENHANCE YOUR CAPACITY

When we consider pilots, what they rarely discuss is how many houses they have built or the balance of their bank accounts. Instead, they often talk about the number of hours they have spent in the air. The more hours they log, the more they get familiar with the various atmospheric conditions above.

What distinguishes a pilot from a captain? Typically, it is someone who has accumulated ten thousand hours or more of flight time. This demonstrates their experience and ability to discern differences in atmospheric conditions, such as when the sun disappears and humidity increases, or when rain is imminent and precautions for landing are necessary.

Like pilots, individuals who have spent considerable time in prayer become adept at navigating the spiritual realm. They dedicate countless hours to communing with God, becoming attuned to shifts in the spiritual atmosphere. Just as Jesus called upon his disciples to join him at prayer times, these prayer warriors recognize the importance of gathering in God's presence.

Matthew 26:40-43 (NLT): **"Then he returned to the disciples and found them asleep. He said to Peter,**

"Couldn't you watch with me even one hour? Keep watch and pray, so that you will not give in to temptation. For the spirit is willing, but the body is weak…!"

Jesus may have been disheartened by his disciples' lack of availability during such a crucial moment in their lives. He probably thought to himself: "My disciples failed to comprehend the solution I had prepared to address their needs." We learn and grow through obedience.

Therefore, they may have struggled to grasp the deeper revelation behind his invitation.

How can one expect to grow in prayer if they do not seize every opportunity to pray that comes their way? God desired for them to suppress their fleshly desires and allow their spirits to prevail.

Unfortunately, their flesh dominated, and they succumbed to deep sleep at an inopportune moment.

Throughout God's word, we see passionate men of prayer facing various situations and bringing victory to many. They often demonstrated diligence and urgency in addressing problems as they arose through prayer.

A good example is provided by the prophet Daniel, who learned how all the wise men of Babylon were to be killed if the explanation of the dream that the king received was not given. He decided to set aside a serious period of prayer and fasting. Let us now consider how Daniel addresses the

king: **"And it is a rare thing that the king requireth, and there is none other that can shew it before the king, except the gods, whose dwelling is not with flesh…» Then Daniel went in, and desired of the king that he would give him time, and that he would shew the king the interpretation. Then Daniel went to his house, and made the thing known to Hananiah, Mishael, and Azariah, his companions: That they would desire mercies of the God of heaven concerning this secret; that Daniel and his fellows should not perish with the rest of the wise men of Babylon. Then was the secret revealed unto Daniel in a night vision. Then Daniel blessed the God of heaven. Daniel answered and said, Blessed be the name of God for ever and ever: for wisdom and might are his: And he changeth the times and the seasons: he removeth kings, and setteth up kings: he giveth wisdom unto the wise, and knowledge to them that know understanding."**
Daniel 2:11; 16-21 (KJV)

Abraham fervently sought a child from God for over 25 years, but God sought a father from many nations.

Similarly, Hannah pleaded with the Lord for a child, but God did not grant her request merely because He needed a child. Instead, He allowed her to reach a point where she could bear a child according to His timing. Hannah's son was destined to become a prophet, serving a greater purpose in leading Israel. Thus, the birth of her son was less about fulfilling her personal desire for a child and more about bringing forth the prophet who would play a significant role in Israel's history.

Choose to cherish your prayer life, for God delights in your prayers. Each prayer session is an opportunity to create, to discern your destiny, and to navigate your path forward. When you trust in God, earthly time (chronos) yields to divine timing (kairos), and the light of the Father envelops you, causing you to shine brightly.

Prepare yourself for a significant outpouring of the Spirit by committing to prayer. Approach the Father with an intensity and fervor like never before, as if each prayer were your final opportunity. Prayer is a powerful force that brings about change. Utilize your knees to chart the course of your life and shape your future in alignment with God's Word.

Through prayer and worship, we cultivate and prepare ourselves for our Kairos moments—those divine, appointed times ordained by God. His faithfulness is unwavering, and His word is steadfastly reliable.

CONCLUSION

This book beautifully captures the profound realities of the Kingdom of God through the ministry of the Holy Spirit and the illuminating Word of God. It delves into the mystery of prayer, exploring the deeper dimensions of the intimate relationship between the Father and His children, harmonized by the sacrificial love of the cross.

These moments within the prayer corridor are truly refreshing, as they emphasize God as our Father, who listens attentively when we call upon Him. The exploration of His attributes ignites a flame within us, fueling our passion for spending quality time in His presence (Shekinah). Moses, revered as a man who conversed with God face to face, serves as a powerful example.

He spent forty days and forty nights on the mountaintop, being an honored guest in God's presence.

Exodus 34:28 (KJV) : **"And he was there with the LORD forty days and forty nights; he neither eat bread, nor drink water. And he wrote upon the tables the words of the covenant, the ten commandments. Now it was so,**

when Moses came down from Mount Sinai (and the two tablets of the Testimony were in Moses' hand when he came down from the mountain), that Moses did not know that the skin of his face shone while he talked with Him."

He indeed spent time conversing with El Shaddai, our Father and the sovereign ruler of the universe. Beyond God, there is only God—He reigns alone, with no other above Him. It brings great joy to know that the Almighty, seated on His majestic throne, delights in the words uttered by the righteous.

I recall an incredible anecdote shared by one of my pastors. He cherished spending time with his family, particularly his daughter. One day, during their time together, his daughter was leading the conversation. After a while, she noticed her father's lack of responsiveness and promptly ceased speaking. Concerned, she asked: "Dad, did you hear what I just said?"

She persisted, urging her father to look at her. Despite reassuring her, the pastor realized a valuable lesson that day. He learned that true listening involves more than just hearing; it requires giving undivided attention and actively engaging with the speaker's words.

Indeed, God's ways are profound, and His plans are beyond human comprehension unless the Holy Spirit opens our eyes to understand them. Often, I ponder the mystery of how God can simultaneously assist all those who pray.

Prayer is indeed a journey marked by love, reverence for God's presence, and dedicated time with the One to whom the entire universe belongs— the One who establishes standards and oversees the cosmos.

Let us approach prayer with enthusiasm, continually seeking God's guidance and intervention. This is a call to prayer—a call to kneel before the Almighty, to influence our generation and those beyond.

When we intercede for those trapped in the darkness of doubt, uncertainty, or confusion, God can shine His light upon their path, bringing clarity and breathing new life into their weary souls.

Each time we extend hospitality, demonstrate care, and maintain a steadfast prayer life, let us ensure that our aspirations align with divine principles. In doing so, we will consistently produce the desired outcomes through our prayers.

Prayer serves as the conduit through which the spiritual realm influences the physical world, unveiling the father's glory and granting our petitions. When we pray, our focus aligns with divine purposes.

Hence, one of the keys to mastering spiritual realities lies in understanding the principles of prayer. Life extends beyond the visible realm; it is inherently spiritual. To bring the invisible into the visible, one must grasp the essence of

PRAYER and remain steadfast in prayerful commitment, for God delights in our prayers.

Do not pray because others are praying or because you feel obligated to do so. And when you do not receive the desired outcome, refrain from becoming discouraged and labeling your experience.

The devil is a liar and the father of liars. The apostle says: "The effectual fervent prayer of a righteous man availeth much..." James 5:16 (KJV)

Prayer holds significant importance in shaping our destiny, yet many people pray without fully comprehending its depth and significance. Often, believers overlook the pivotal role of prayer in guiding their destinies.

When faced with challenges or when our will clashes with the Father's will, it is crucial to reflect on relevant passages of Scripture for guidance and understanding. These scriptures serve as guiding lights, illuminating our path, and aligning our hearts with the will of God. **"Now therefore thus saith the LORD of hosts; Consider your ways. Ye have sown much, and bring in little; ye eat, but ye have not enough; ye drink, but ye are not filled with drink; ye clothe you, but there is none warm; and he that earneth wages earneth wages to put it into a bag with holes. Thus saith the LORD of hosts; Consider your ways."** Haggai 1:5-7 (KJV)

There may be aspects that remain unexplored or not fully grasped as you seek to fulfill your purpose on Earth. It is imperative to search your heart and repent, opening yourself to new revelations and deeper understanding of prayer.

With this newfound insight into the profound dimensions of prayer, let us establish a solid foundation for a prayer-centered Christian life.

Through prayer, we can live victoriously and fulfill our earthly mandate. Remember, the obstacle does not lie with God; it often stems from humanity's shortcomings. God offers Himself to assist us and is always available to listen. Engage in prayer now, and you will be astonished by the results.

O THOU THAT HEARETH PRAYER

Let us harness the power of prayer to unlock endless possibilities.

From the dawn of creation, God has cherished human fellowship. Since the moment He formed Adam and Eve, He delighted in spending time with them. Our understanding of God as an attentive listener shapes our devotional practices, transforming prayer into a ministry of devotion.

ABOUT THE AUTHOR

Pastor Alain Lubamba spearheads all outreach initiatives, church planting endeavors, expansion projects, and mission activities for Divine Grace Gathering Church in Canada and globally. With a fervent passion for God and a deep commitment to prayer, he is revered as a dedicated servant of Christ.

Having served in various leadership capacities and ministries for many years, Pastor Alain Lubamba is recognized as a soul-winner and a seasoned revivalist. His journey in ministry spans from youth ministry at Centre Evangelique et Francophone La Borne in the DRC to his current pastoral role at DGG.

A devoted follower of Christ, Pastor Alain Lubamba exemplifies a life grounded in prayer and faith. He has personally witnessed the transformative power of God, empowering believers to lead victorious and fulfilling lives daily.

Pastor Alain Lubamba's academic achievements include a degree in theology and Bible studies, a master's degree in finance, and several other diplomas, reflecting his commitment to both spiritual and intellectual growth.